Theo-
logy
&
Life

THEOLOGY AND LIFE SERIES

One Bread and Cup

Source of Communion

by

Ernest R. Falardeau, S.S.S.

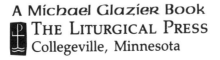

A Michael Glazier Book
THE LITURGICAL PRESS
Collegeville, Minnesota

About the Author

ERNEST R. FALARDEAU, S.S.S., holds a doctorate in sacred theology from the Gregorian University and a master of science in library science from (Case) Western Reserve University. He is associate pastor, St. Charles Borromeo Church, Albuquerque, N.M., and serves as chairman for the Commission for Ecumenical and Interfaith Affairs, archdiocese of Santa Fe. He has published articles in *Emmanuel, Priest,* and *Review for Religious.*

A Michael Glazier Book

published by

THE LITURGICAL PRESS

Cover design by Lillian Brulc.

2   3   4   5   6   7   8   9

Library of Congress Cataloging-in-Publication Data

Falardeau, Ernest R.
    One bread and cup : source of communion / by Ernest R. Falardeau.
      p.   cm.
    "A Michael Glazier book."
    Reprint. Originally published: Wilmington, Del. : M. Glazier, 1987. (Theology and life series ; v. 19).
    Includes bibliographical references and index.
    ISBN 0-8146-5614-5
    1. Lord's Supper—Catholic Church. 2. Catholic Church—Doctrines. 3. Spiritual life—Catholic authors. 4. Close and open communion. 5. Lord's Supper and Christian union. I. Title. II. Series: Theology and life series ; v. 19.
BX2235.F34   1990
234'.163—dc20

90-19320
CIP

Contents

Preface

Eucharistic spirituality is the study of the experience of God in the celebration, reception and prayerful contemplation of the memorial (anamnesis) which the Lord Jesus left to his Church as the sacrifice and symbol of God's love "unto the end" (Jn 13:1). As the source and center of the Christian life, the Eucharist is of special interest for those who study and live the life of Christ.

Ours is an ecumenical study because we wish to draw deeply and frequently not only from Catholic sources and Vatican II documents, but also from the experience and writings of other Christians. We focus particularly on the ecumenical bi-lateral and multi-lateral writings which have emerged in the last dozen years and which move theology and the churches to a new high ground from which to view the Christian message and the future of the Church.

Spirituality as a theological discipline is developing along with the rest of theology. It is influenced by systematic theology, biblical studies, church history, ecumenism, and related fields of psychology, anthropology, and social science. It is not our intention to be academic, but pastoral. Yet we hope to steer a middle course between the two.

It is becoming increasingly clear in the wake of Vatican II that the Church is the laity. Their numbers, their growing expertise and their commitment make them extremely important to the future of the Church. We write for them as well as for their leaders whether lay, religious or clerical. We are particularly hopeful that they will appreciate the scholarship of this study as well as our pastoral concern.

*   *   *   *   *

We are grateful to many who assisted us over the years in preparing for this work. In particular we thank the faculty of the Gregorian University in Rome who prepared us through its doctoral program. The Congregation of the Blessed Sacrament, especially its General Administration and Provincial Council has been supportive of our ecumenical ministry, for which we are grateful. Many colleagues in several Orthodox, Catholic and Protestant churches especially in the New Mexico Conference of Churches and the National Association of Diocesan Ecumenical Officers (NADEO) have inspired and moved us ecumenically; our special thanks to them. To secretarial staff, especially Margaret Mulder, and to publisher Michael Glazier who guided us in our work, we express our deep appreciation.

Ernest Falardeau, S.S.S.

Introduction

Karl Rahner called Vatican II a copernican revolution in the Church.[1] It really was. The center of that revolution is the new ecclesiology reflected in *Lumen Gentium* and *Gaudium et Spes*. Like Copernicus' view that the sun was the center of the solar system and not the earth, so the new view that the Mystical Body of Christ is the center of the Church. If the Church is a "communion of communions,"[2] our immediate task is to see ourselves as part of a whole, not the whole itself. In such a perception of things we have much to learn from other churches and communions. But more importantly our perception of ourselves and our Church and our Christian life is radically altered.

To understand eucharistic spirituality today we need to understand Church and Eucharist. Spirituality flows from our understanding of Church, and not the reverse.

[1]Karl Rahner. *Concern For The Church:* Theological Investigations XX Transl. by Edward Quinn. N.Y. Crossroad, 1981. esp. Part Four: Future of the Church p. 77-186.

[2]J. Robert Wright. *A Communion of Communions:* One Eucharistic Fellowship (survey of the ecumenical relationhips of the Episcopal Church). N.Y. Seabury Press, 1979.

The New Church

Since Vatican II the Catholic Church has been involved in extensive ecumenical dialogue. Early in these dialogues it became evident that a new language and theology would be needed if the dialogue was to get beyond the repetition of polemical positions of the past.[3] Differences in theology needed to be separated from differences in doctrine.[4] This ecumenical atmosphere is giving birth to a new theology, a new language to describe the consensus in faith which is shared across church lines.

One of the most important realities about which a theological consensus has been reached is the notion of Church. The Church is the people of God. Born again in Baptism as members of Christ's Body by faith and grace, Christians share the same hope and eternal destiny. Thus the Church is one because it is a family of God's children.

The Church shares Christ's mission to save the world by spreading the good news of salvation. This message of "good news" is spread by Christian witness, the evidence of daily living "in Christ" for the world. The Church as people, baptized, and sharing the mission of Jesus to save the world, is the core reality of our faith. In this perception of things the Church is one. Its divisions are an accident of history, not the substance of its existence. What God united , men should never have divided. And yet such is the case. Over 300 different Churches profess to be the Church of Christ. Yet not many of them are willing to admit their neighbors are also the Church of Christ. Nevertheless, such *recognition* is at the heart of the ecumenical movement. Until we recognize the existence, Baptism, Ministry and Eucharist of other

---

[3]ARCIC I. *The Final Report*. Preface, p. 2 and Eucharistic Doctrine Elucidation #4 and 5.

[4]Paul C. Empie. *Lutherans and Catholics in Dialogue:* Personal Notes and Study. Ed. by Raymond Tremeyer. Philadelphia. Fortress Press 1981.

Churches, we have not reached the first level of ecumenical unity.[5] This book will need over and again to suggest that genuine eucharistic spirituality today will need to understand the Church in an ecumenical way. We need to pray and work toward recognition of ministries and sacraments. Eucharistic spirituality today rests on the hope that some day the unity which is ours in faith will be celebrated in Eucharist.[6]

The New Eucharist

There was a time when the Eucharist was seen as the priest's offering of the Sacrifice of Calvary in an unbloody way. It was the priest's action, offered for the sake of the people. Rather than something celebrated, the Eucharist was something said or sung. The problem of something that was "once and for all (ephapax)" (Heb 10:12,18), and repeatedly offered was not fully resolved.

Vatican II theology changed this perception. The concept of *"anamnesis,"*—something not merely "remembered," but memorialized (i.e., actually shared here and now)—found wide acceptance everywhere.[7] The notion of sacrifice was understood to mean the one, same sacrifice is now shared through the Eucharist. The need to repeat was not because the Sacrifice was insufficient, but because men and women

[5]W.C.C. *Baptism, Eucharist and Ministry.* See also Max Thurian, ed. *Ecumenical Perspectives On Baptism, Eucharist and Ministry.* Geneva, W.C.C. 1983. (Faith and Order Paper #116.)

[6]W.C.C. General Assembly. Vancouver, July 1983. See also Faith and Order Conference, Montreal 1963.

[7]Michael Schmaus. *Teologia Dogmatica.* Edicion al cuidado de Lucio Garcia Ortega y Raimundo Drudis Baldrich; revision teologica del M.I. Sr. D. Jose M. Caballero Cuesta. Madrid, Rialp SA, 1960 8v. v. 6 Los Sacramentos #254 El sacrificio eucaristico, el sacrificio de cruz y la iglesia. p. 331-388. [orig. *Katholisce Dogmatik.* München, Max Hueber, 1957.]

are born and they die. They must be saved individually and daily. The Lord's "daily bread" must be eaten frequently to conquer one's "daily sins," and our basic sinfulness. No longer preoccupied with the need for something *new* in the Eucharist, we can now concentrate on how the mystery of Christ is shared through the Sacrament.

The Eucharist is the people's action *(leitos ergon)*[8] Liturgy is the prayer/offering of Jesus Christ for the people. It is also their acceptance of his Sacrifice, their prayer and their offering together with Christ. Not as though Christ's prayer or offering were insufficient or incomplete. But Christians make their own what Christ offered. Christ offers as the head of the Mystical Body; Christians offer as members of that same Body.

The prayer of Christ for us is eternal and efficacious (Heb 10:11-15), but our prayer needs to be made daily. Prayer opens our minds and hearts to God. Without our effort salvation cannot take place.

The Eucharist is communion (koinonia) with Jesus and with the members of his Body. This concept of communion is central to our understanding of Eucharist.[9] Jesus is present *for* us. He needs to be present *with* us.[10] That is, we must be present to him. Without such openness on our part, there can be no fruitful communion; indeed there can be no communion at all.

The New Spirituality

A spirituality may be defined as the particular way in which a Christian incarnates the Gospel in his or her per-

[8]Cyprian Vagaggini, O.S.B. *Theological Dimensions of the Liturgy*. Collegeville, MN, The Liturgical Press, 1959.......vols. II *Senso Teologico della Liturgia*. Roma, Ed. Paoline, 1959.

[9]See ARCIC. *The Final Report*. Introd. #6 and Eucharistic Doctrine #6-9 and Elucidation #7.

[10]ARCIC I. *The Final Report*. Par. #8. See also—J.M.R. Tillard, O.P. passim.

sonal life.[11] Spirituality may be called living theology. It involves all the elements of the Christian life worked into a personal and practical synthesis for daily living. At the heart of a spirituality is the Gospel and its incorporation in the individual through grace. Also involved are the personal values, perceptions, and ideals of the individual. The Christian message is perceived in different ways at different times by different individuals. In a lifetime one might conceivably alter one's spirituality considerably due to one's own growth and perception as well as due to changes in the cultural world in which one lives. St. Peter Julian Eymard passed from a spirituality largely characterized by the French School of Spirituality to a much more Salesian orientation at the end of his life.[12] The latter change was due to his later development of a eucharistic spirituality which emphasized much more the virtue of charity rather than the French or Berullian School's emphasis on the virtue of religion.

The twelfth century obviously had a great influence on Francis of Assisi's spirituality, just as the sixteenth had an influence on Carmelite and Jesuit spirituality. All of the cultural influences which affect an individual: theology, secular and church history, cultural trends, family background, education—all influence spirituality.

In this context the influence of Vatican II on our personal spirituality is beyond measure. Depending upon how much each individual has absorbed the spirit of the Council, one's spirituality reflects that spirit or not. Our conviction is that openness to the Holy Spirit working through the Council is essential to holiness in our time.[13] One ignores the Council and the Spirit who guided it at one's own peril. If holiness

[11]For works on Spirituality see A. Royo, O.P., and J. Aumann, O.P. *The Theology of Christian Perfection.* Dubuque, Priory Press 1962.

[12]Eugenio Nunez, S.S.S. *La Spiritualité. du P. Pierre-Julien Eymard.* Rome, Congregation du T.S. Sacrement, 1956.

[13]Ladislas Örsy. *Open To The Spirit.* Religious Life After Vatican II. Washington, DC, Corpus Books, 1968.

can be identified with following the guidance of the Holy Spirit, or letting the Spirit work in our lives, then being open to the Spirit is imperative.

Catholic spirituality today must be ecumenical and eucharistic because the Vatican Council was ecumenical and eucharistic. The renewal of the Church requires a new understanding of Church and a greater awareness of the role of the Eucharist in the life of the Church. The Eucharist must reflect and celebrate a life that is transformed by the gospel. These are the characteristics of every Christian's spirituality today.

As an ecumenical spirituality, Christian spirituality reflects the new understanding that the Church is universal and embodies all Christians, not simply one Church. Working and praying for the unity of the Church becomes a way of life, not a hobby or avocation. Learning from other Christians and their perception of the Gospel is also fruitful. Working with other Christians for the betterment of the world is seen as a fulfillment of the mission of Christ by Christians. Dialoguing for a better understanding of one's own faith is also useful. Spiritual ecumenism is both possible and necessary for today's Christian.

As a eucharistic spirituality, Christian living centers on the underlying understanding of what the Eucharist is. A sign of Christ's love for his Church, the Eucharist is the focus of the Christian's response to Christ's love. It is a challenge to love of neighbor, since that is the hallmark of the Christian's love for the Lord.

As a sign of the forgiveness of sin, the Eucharist deepens our separation from sin and attachment to God. It challenges us to forgive as we are forgiven. It is thus a sign of peace and reconciliation in a world fraught with the danger of war and nuclear annihilation.

The Eucharist is the celebration of the life of the Church. People participate in the Liturgy because they share in the life of the Church. Liturgy is the solemn celebration of Christ, head and members. It is the joyful remembrance of the paschal mystery, a proclamation of the good news of the

Gospel, a liberation from sin and fear of death, a communion with God and neighbor.[14]

In this work we will concentrate on the Eucharist as Communion. But one facet of the Eucharist always implies and calls for the other aspects of the Bread of Life. We cannot say everything about the Eucharist, yet it is important we do not divide what is truly one in this Sacrament.

The Future of Christian Spirituality

We can only live one life at a time. Tomorrow will have its own spirituality. But the future of Christian spirituality will be deeply influenced by the Council and what we live through today. Our spirituality today is influenced by Francis of Assisi, Teresa of Avila, John of the Cross, Ignatius of Loyola and Peter Julian Eymard. The Catholic who develops a spirituality in the year 2000 will be influenced by what happens to the Church today. Particularly significant is the Second Vatican Council, one of the most far-reaching in its doctrine of all the ecumenical councils, and its influence on Christians.

As we develop the fundamental ideas of this book around the Eucharist and the unity of the Church, we will better appreciate the watershed that Vatican II represents. Catholic spirituality will never be the same after this historic breakthrough. Not only the Liturgy has been influenced, but every aspect of the Church's life and mission. Our task is to focus on the theological and spiritual implications of the great teachings of the Council. We hope thereby to assist many in the development of a way of living the Gospel that is in tune with the Spirit and a cause of great joy and peace.

[14]Eugene La Verdiere, S.S.S. *Eucharist: Proclamation, Liberation, Communion.* Several articles published in *Emmanuel* and reprinted in N.Y. by Sentinel Press.

1

The Laity, the Church and the Eucharist

It is almost trite to describe Vatican II as the Council of the emerging layman.[1] And yet, because that emerging is so important to the Church's self-understanding and the development of Catholic spirituality in our time, we need to draw special and considerable attention to this aspect of Christian living.

The Spirituality of the Laity

Besides emphasizing the necessity of lay involvement in every aspect of Christian living and of the mission of the Church, Vatican II stressed that the laity are called to the very heights of Christian holiness. The Council clarified that there were not two spiritualities, one for the clergy and the

[1]Donald J. Thorman. *The Emerging Layman:* the Role of the Catholic Layman in America. Garden City, Doubleday, 1962.

other for the laity. There is only one pattern or way to holiness: by imitating the love of Christ for God and human beings. Being a Christian is simply the incarnation of Christ's love in us. "For me to live is Christ" (Phil 1:21) expresses what it means to be a Christian.

The Council explains[2] that each of us becomes holy by living the Christian vocation in the context of our individual call, whatever that call may be. The cobbler becomes holy by repairing shoes and living as a Christian. His dealings with people and his sanctification of labor and transformation of the world is wrapped up in his work as well as his prayer. The monk is not an island cut off from the rest of the continent. His prayer must include and affect the social concerns and problems of men and women in the world around him. He is called to pray and to work for the elimination of poverty, discrimination and injustice. The context for his efforts are different from those of the statesman, but he shares basically the same mission.

Before we can express the distinctness of the spirituality of the laity, we must be able to see it in the context of the universal call to holiness in the Church. This approach is reflected in the Dogmatic Constitution on the Church (*Lumen Gentium*).[3]

What distinguishes lay spirituality is its secularity. The layman/laywoman is called to live, work and be holy "in the world," i.e., as a part of the distinctly secular world in which they live. The clergy work in the context of the Church.

Efforts to blur this distinction are made at times, and there are those who feel such a distinction is not useful in our time. Harvey Cox in *"The Secular City"*[4] makes a strong case against the distinction of secular and sacred. The call of the Bible is to sacralize the secular city. Teilhard de Char-

---

[2]*Lumen Gentium* #40. *Gaudium et Spes* #35, 38.

[3]*Lumen Gentium.* Ch. 4. The Laity. Ch. 5. The Call of the Whole Church to Holiness.

[4]Harvey Cox. *The Secular City.* N.Y. Macmillan 1965.

din's approach would concur.[5] The Holy Father's involvement in human rights, and the several national conferences of bishops speaking out on social questions seem to blur some of these distinctions.

And yet the Code of Canon Law and the constant policy of Rome are against political involvement.[6] The Holy Father, as an astute student of political principle and practice, wishes the lines to be clear and distinct between Church and State. When the Church speaks it must be as the arbiter of justice and peace and the moral conscience of society. The Church should not be involved in politics.

In this respect, the lay person differs from the cleric. The laity should be involved in the secular city since that is their calling. The churchman should not be involved in business, the lay man or woman must do so to earn a living. The place of the clergy is in the church or rectory; the place of the laity is in the marketplace.[7]

The Council suggests we clearly define the role of laity and clergy. This is ultimately to clearly unite them in the one mission of the Church. This is not to say that one is called to holiness and the other is not. Rather it underscores there is a different *way* in which laity and clergy strive and achieve the perfection of their Christian way of life.

Pope John XXIII[8] spoke of "convivenza" as the other side of reform in the Church. *Aggiornamento* is simply updating, making structures that are inefficient or inept disappear in favor of structures that are more productive. He described *convivenza* as the process by which the living and preaching of the Gospel penetrates and affects every aspect of human life: education, family life, culture, science, industry, politics,

[5]Esp. Pierre Teilhard de Chardin. *The Divine Milieu: an essay on the interior life.* [1st ed.] N.Y. Harper, 1960.

[6]Code of Canon Law. c.285 #3.

[7]See *Lumen Gentium* #31.

[8]Bernard R. Bonnot, *Pope John XXIII: An Astute, Pastoral Leader.* New York, Alba House, 1968. XXII, 315p. See esp. p. 107-139.

etc. Clergy and laity must be concerned with *convivenza.*
The clergy exercise their role of service and leadership so as
to raise the consciousness of the laity to their task in society.
Preaching the word and administering the sacraments is the
way in which clergy become holy. Working at the structures
and inner-workings of society and at the relationships of
people among themselves is the way in which the laity develop Christian holiness. Whether one plays the violin, legis-
lates in city, state or national assemblies, works in an office,
shop or factory, the lay person is expected to act as a leaven
to raise the level of society to that of the kingdom of God.

Modern eschatology[9] either interprets the kingdom as
begun in this world or entirely future in the world to come.
(Those who interpret the kingdom as of/in this world
entirely, have a difficult time reconciling such a concept with
Jesus' explicit statement to the contrary.) Building the city of
God in the city of man has been a graphic description of
Christianity since the time of Augustine.

The Universal Call to Holiness

If there is one call to holiness which the laity share with
the clergy, how in practice does holiness develop for the
laity? We have already stressed that the holiness of the laity
is exercised in the world and within one's special call or
vocation as a lay person.

This holiness is also not different from that of the clergy in
that it is a universal call to charity. Love of God and neighbor are the great commandments and also the acid test of
one's growth in Christ. "If we say that we love God, but do
not keep his commandments, we are liars" (1 Jn 3:20). In the

[9]Eschatology is the theology of the end of the world or history.
The *eschata* (final things) are heaven, hell, purgatory, judgment,
final resurrection, etc. For an interesting discussion of the effect of
eschatology on ecclesiology see Carl E. Braaten "Ecumenical
Dimensions of the Expanding Church-State Challenge" (unpublished address to NADEO, April 20, 1982, Grand Rapids, MI.)

Sermon on the Mount Jesus described "perfection" in the Christian life as imitating the Father. Just as the Father is even-handed in his blessings of sun and rain, so should Christians be even-handed in their love of friend and foe (cf. Mt 5:43-48).

Love and Marriage

Augustine's pessimism has been described as an outgrowth of his Manichaeism. Some of that pessimism penetrated Western Chrisitianity through his writings and his influence.[10] The Manichaeans were opposed to marriage, and even more to sex. Celibacy was seen as a more "pure" form of life. While marriage and celibacy are regarded as acceptable ways of achieving holiness in eastern Christianity, in the West they are not given practical currency as equals. The Christian tradition favors celibacy as a greater sign of the kingdom. We are not questioning that preference here, but we suggest that such a preference and the pessimism which has surrounded marriage in the West, have not led to a view that one can achieve equal levels of holiness in either state. Whatever one may say about the matter theoretically, the practical perception of western laity is that marriage and celibacy are not in any way equal.

We do not intend to resolve here the question of the Roman Catholic requirement of celibacy for ordination to the priesthood. However, the lack of genuine option in this matter seems to obscure the basic tenet that all are called to the one holiness and that vocation is the determining factor about the *way* in which one lives out the Christian call. Paul does not impose celibacy on his hearers/readers; "let him who can take it do so" was the Lord's injunction which Paul repeats (Mt 19:12; I Cor 7:32-35).

[10]The concept of Augustinian pessimism was developed in a course by Fr. A. Liuima, S.J., in a doctoral course at the Gregorian Univ. in 1958.

We are in a changing world. Instant communication from every corner of the world, churches in dialogue and uniting, celibate clergy meeting and admiring and working with married clergy, biblical insights on a new and changing scene, and many other social, cultural and religious factors make it impossible to predict the future. To think the "enclaves" of any church can remain immune to the tremendous ferment of the times and the inspiration of the Spirit, is to be both naive and spiritually immature. Religious values are perhaps the very last to change. When side by side history places an immobile Church (change was almost nil for 450 years in all churches) and an exploding cultural matrix, we readily perceive the stuff of which religious tensions are made. The present conservative/fundamentalist trend cannot survive a technologically expanding world. Our giant thinkers and "prophets" point to the need for religious development that will parallel a world about to move into the post-space age.

Our religious perception of marriage must come to grips with the sexual revolution. We do not mean that "everything goes" should be the rule. We have reaped the whirlwind of such a pattern. But the victorian prudery of the past must give way to the genuine insights of sound psychology, and rigid efforts "to keep the genie in the box" must yield to a more enlightened realization that such efforts are futile and unchristian. The basic premise of Christianity is incarnational and resurrectional. God became human to raise humanity to its rightful and God-given dignity. God created a world in which everything is good...including sex, love and marriage. Lust is a sin; love is a virtue. Sex is neutral; its use is to be governed by love, not by lust. It is imperative that we finally put to rest the manichaean ogre that would not give marriage its rightful beauty as a Sacrament and sign of God's covenant with his people.

Orthodoxy is the thin line between extremes. Chesterton[11] indicated that the genius of Catholicism has been the ability

---

[11]Gilbert Keith Chesterton. *Orthodoxy*. London, Bradley Head, 1949, p. 278. The Paradoxes of Christianity, p. 131-169.

to walk the thin line of orthodoxy throughout the centuries. Yet this balance needs constantly to be renewed with every age. Indeed our age makes special demands on the flexibility of Catholic Christianity because it is an age of such tremendous and such rapid change.

In the area of marriage, we are still in need of a balanced and complete theology. We are too near both the victorian era and the sexual revolution to fully appreciate the delicate balance needed on this subject. Our dialogue with Orthodox, Anglican, Lutheran and Protestant theology will help us to shape that balance. Marriage and celibacy are found side by side in the ranks of clergy and laity. Religious dedication also is found within and without all ranks of the Church. This has not impoverished the dedication of these Christians, but enhanced it.

Without putting marriage on a pedestal, we must not detract from its beauty and its sacramentality. While exalting religious dedication in celibacy, we must be able to appreciate married clergy not as a lesser call or way, but as a *different* call or way.[12] Each call and way is the work of the Spirit "who breathes as he wills" (Jn 3:8).

Further, it must be admitted that the more common way is that of married life. While Paul calls others to be like himself, he makes this an option. Most people are not called to it. They are called to work out their salvation in the married state, with the challenges it affords. Blessed by God's love, consecrated in Christ by a sacrament, the task of married Christians is to exemplify the love of Christ for his bride, the Church, and of the bride for her Spouse, Christ. Celibacy extols the kingdom to come; marriage the kingdom begun. In the final analysis Paul's exhortation is that each state must be appreciated; neither is to be envied. To each his own, and God's blessings to all.

Without wishing to detract from the sublimity of the celibate state, or to exaggerate the beauty of the married state,

[12]Carolus Vladimirus Truhlar, S.J. *Antonomiae Vitae Spiritualis.* 3a rev. ed. Romae, Pontif. Univ. Gregorianium, 1961. (Collect. Spiritualia, 4).

we would like to say with Vatican II that holiness is for all, whatever their state in life. Holiness is not hampered by the married state. Since this is the call of most of God's people, all of whom are called to be holy, this state too is a holy state.

Within marriage love of husband and wife for each other and their children is the normal avenue for love of God. Families in a neighborhood or parish living similar patterns of Christian living help each other to form the Church, the body of Christ. *Community* building is the crying need of our time. Such community begins at the Eucharist and in the Church, but touches the neighborhood and the world.

For too long, our laity have felt as though sanctity belonged to the clergy or religious. Vatican II rightly set the record straight. Many a cleric must admit to a daily experience of holiness far beyond his own in his pastoral experience. The courage, patience, long-suffering and forgiving spirit of countless lay persons gives daily inspiration to anyone who has eyes to see and ears to hear.

Most importantly the Vatican Council has stressed mutual help and cooperation between the laity and pastors of souls. The laity have a right to expect inspiration and leadership from the clergy in their pursuit of holiness in the imitation of Jesus Christ. The clergy are to serve and facilitate this growth in holiness by providing example and counsel. As Raymond Brown said so well in "*The Churches the Apostles Left Behind*,"[13] the laity need spirituality in the Church:

> "In the Roman Catholic parishes that have taken the changes of Vatican II seriously there is often much more participation of parishioners in liturgy and in parish life in general. It is all the more startling, then, for pastors of such active parishes to find they are losing parishioners to religious groups that stress a personal relationship to Jesus, basing themselves on the Scriptures (sometimes fundamentalistically interpreted). Such pastors will argue

[13]Raymond E. Brown, S.S. *The Churches the Apostles Left Behind*. New York, Paulist Press 1984.

correctly that there cannot be a Church unless there is a worshiping community; but they are finding that worship in itself, without an accompanying personal spirituality, does not hold some people...Nevertheless, I would argue that John (Gospel) has a corrective role to play in the mainline churches when it is read critically rather than harmonistically. It can remind them, as it did Christians in the first century, that Church membership is not a sufficient goal, for the Church must be in a loving relationship to him".[14]

He says further:

"There is a special problem in the churches that have an ordained *priesthood* in their church structure...In relation to the equality of Christians as disciples, it is especially difficult for the ordained priesthood to be kept in the category of service (to God and to the community), for the ordained will frequently be assumed to be more important and automatically more holy. Because ordination is seen as a sacrament and priests deal with sacred things, they are frequently regarded as better than ordinary Christians. In my own church some would find surprising this almost elementary affirmation: the day when a person is baptized is more important than the day when a person was ordained a priest or bishop. The first sacrament, after all, touches on salvation; it constitutes one a child of God, a dignity that goes beyond designation to the special service of God".[15]

He then points out how laudable it would be for a pope to use his baptismal name, rather than another to emphasize "that *salvifically* an identity as a Christian is more important than an identity gained from authority."[16]

[14]Raymond E. Brown, S.S. *The Churches the Apostles Left Behind,* p. 98.

[15]*Ibid.* p. 100.

[16]*Ibid.* p. 100.

Our purpose here is not to belabor the point. It is simply to indicate how difficult it is for the laity to understand their dignity as God's children and their call to holiness in the Church.

Consecrated Celibacy/Virginity and Religious Life

The Vatican Council emphasized the need for the witness of religious life in the Church.[17] It underscored that consecrated virginity/celibacy is a sign of the kingdom to come. In that kingdom they will neither marry nor give in marriage, but be like the angels. (Mt 22:30). It would be useful here to underscore the witness of religious life as a complement to lay holiness. This will highlight its distinctiveness and its similarity to holiness in other vocations.

Vatican II states clearly that there is one form of holiness in the Church, though there are many ways of living it. Holiness consists in living out one's baptism.[18] Living the Gospel, celebrating the mystery of Christ in Sacraments, and developing through prayer an intimate communion with Christ (and the Trinity) are facets of Christian holiness.

We have often heard that the laity live by the commandments, religious live by the beatitudes. That simply is not the kind of distinction that holds up under the Vatican II teachings. All Christians must live both the commandments and the beatitudes. While it might be true that there is a close connection between the public vows of poverty, chastity, and obedience and the beatitudes, yet all the virtues implied must be practiced by lay and religious Christians.

If lay and religious Christians must strive for the same holiness, in what are they different? The best answer seems to be that they differ in the *way* in which they strive for holiness and live the Christian life. This *way* is characterized

---

[17]*Lumen Gentium* #44 and #46. See *Perfectae Caritatis* #1.
[18]*Lumen Gentium* #40.

by the public pronouncement of the vows of poverty (simplicity), chastity (consecrated virginity/celibacy) and obedience.

For St. Benedict the only distinctive element of religious life is the vow of obedience.[19] The other two vows are contained in provisions of the rule (or of Canon Law). Religious obedience places the individual directly under the command of a superior (whatever the name) to whom they are responsible for their actions and for the evaluation of their enterprises.

Sign of the Kingdom

The Council underscores that religious are clear signs of the kingdom to come. But all Christians are such signs. Perhaps the *radical* nature of the sign given by religious is characteristic. In other words, while all Christians must give witness that the kingdom comes, religious do so in a more radical way. This is clearly seen from their vow of virginity/celibacy. To some extent it is also visible in their radical vows of poverty and obedience.

The Council draws attention to the prophetic witness of religious.[20] Throughout the centuries the saintly founders and foundresses of religious institutes have been characterized by their ability to challenge prevalent currents in the Church. They were thus able to give new directions. They were able to recall more fundamental values in the Christian ethos. Prophets in their times are instruments of the Holy Spirit, they are able to begin movements of great holiness and radical reform in the Church. While it is also true that

---

[19]Columba Marmion, O.S.B. *Christ the Ideal of the Monk:* spiritual conferences on the monastic and religious life. 4th ed. N.Y. Herder, 1926. *The Rule of Saint Benedict;* edit. and with an English translation and explanatory notes by D. Oswald Hunter Blair. 5th rev. ed. Fort Augustus, Abbey Press, 1948.

[20]*Lumen Gentium* #44. *Perfectae Caritatis* #14, 20 and 25.

they are products of their time, they are especially products of divine grace and the Spirit's call.

Religious are called to be prophetic by virtue of their baptism. But their heritage and vocation calls them to a more radical and sustained prophetic witness. When others in the Church might be content to go along with the tide of trends, religious are called to be consistent reminders to Christians that "we have not here a lasting city."

This prophetic call should be present in the dealings of religious with the hierarchy.[21] The tendency of the hierarchy is to see in religious the many hands and feet needed for ministry. Religious need to recall that their ministry transcends the local Church, and is most effective when it ministers its own special charism to the local Church and beyond.

Religious bear witness to the laity of the kingdom to come. Their love for Christ can be an inspiration to the laity. The love of husbands and wives can inspire the dedication of religious to the Church and the people religious serve.

Single people in the world can see in religious the possibility of dedication in celibate life to Christ and the kingdom. Service to people can become a goal and way of life for them in the world, as it is for religious in the cloister.

Religious and Secularity

We are living in an age of great secularization. Religious must often ask themselves whether their task is to be a part of the secularizing trend (can they do otherwise?), or a force for sacralizing the secular. Harvey Cox is often quoted as favoring a secularizing of the city. Our reading of his message is rather that there is a need to sacralize a world that is becoming secular by its own technological and materialistic weight.[22] The kingdom is built *in this world* even though it is

[21]John Paul II "I have recently"—Address to some U.S. Bishops. Sept. 19, 1983. *The Pope Speaks* 28 (1983) 344-349.

[22]See Harvey Cox. *The Secular City*; secularization and urbani-

built by people who are *not of this world,* i.e., are deeply spiritual.

In an article on liberation theology U.S. style which appeared in *America* in the spring of 1985,[23] a modern author suggests that we should explore our own spiritual heritage in America, rather than import theologies from abroad. He suggests that we might follow the example of Martin Luther King, Jr. who stated during the march on Washington, D.C. that he had come to cash a check, a promissory note that freedom would be granted to blacks. He appealed to the moral conscience of his fellow citizens and the fundamental principles of freedom and equal justice which are the foundation of our American experiment.

Similarly we religious Americans need not be ashamed of what we have learned from 200 years of the American experiment. John Courtney Murray was able to see in the American experiment an ideal for exportation to the universal Church, rather than an isolated case to be submerged beneath the weight of the European tradition. We have yet much to learn from our heritage of freedom, truth, fairplay and open relations.[24]

I am suggesting that the living of religious life in America may yet write a page in the history of the Church that will be an example for generations to come. American woman especially, having shared both the freedom and equality which our laws guarantee (the right to free speech, and personal choice), may yet point the way in the Church for full use of the gifts and charism of religious women.

zation in theological perspective. N.Y. Macmillan 1965. VIII, 276 p. esp. p. 18-36 and 125-162.

[23]Russell Barta. "Liberation: U.S. Style." *America.* Vol 152 p. 297-300, April 13, 1985.

[24]See Christopher F. Mooney. *Religion and the American Dream:* the Search for Freedom Under God. Philadelphia, Westminster, c. 1977. See also Archbishop Rembert G. Weakland, O.S.B. *All God's People:* Catholic Identity After the Second Vatican Council. N.Y. Paulist, 1985. 206 p. esp. p. 173-206.

The pluralism of our religious experience gave birth to Vatican II's decree on religious freedom. That experience can point the way to genuine ecumenical relations in openness, freedom of expression, genuine search for truth and treatment of others as equals.

Augustinian pessimism of every shape and color so dominates our spiritual theology, that it is extremely difficult to fully develop the incarnational/resurrectional spirituality which is at the core of the Christian message. In the area of human development, there is yet much to be changed before we reach the point where "grace building on nature" becomes the foundation of Christian spirituality in practice as well as in theory.

The social sciences, especially psychology, are telling us that genuine human development is being hampered by the excessive and compulsive guilt which people are heaping upon themselves in our time. The rate of suicide is mounting every day—a sign of the malaise that exists. If we preach a Gospel of mercy and forgiveness, we must develop a spirituality of human development based on confidence in God, trust in his word, and faith in his grace.

The theology of Karl Rahner, especially his rich spirituality is a mine yet to be thoroughly explored. Rahner's faith is in a world redeemed, and in expanding possibilities for human development through the grace of God. Holiness is wholeness. It cannot exist fully except where the human potential is given wings, and the possibility of development.

The Eucharist as Liberation

It is in this context that the Eucharist as liberation figures. The Eucharist has been described by Leo XIII as the extension of the Incarnation.[25] Jesus became Saviour so that we might be set free from sin and from all that would make us

---

[25]Leo XIII, Pope. *Mirae Caritatis* Dz. 3360.

less human. Through the Eucharist we share in the divine life of the Father through Jesus and in the Spirit.

Free from sin and alive for God through the Eucharist, we daily become more fully children of God. The God of creation re-creates in us the divine life which was full in Jesus. Repairing and renewing human nature, building upon it, grace matures us after the example of the perfect man, Jesus. We do not become fully Christian on our own, but by the grace of God. Our full human potential and our full Christian development are made possible by the Risen Lord who becomes our Bread of Life.

The Mission of the Church and the Laity

Through Baptism every lay person shares in the mission of Christ, the mission of the Church.[26] Proclaiming the Gospel to every creature, building the kingdom, in the context of Vatican II means more than preaching. It is the witness of life, and involves the transformation of the world. This task of changing the world also involves the transformation of structures that tend to make people less human, or prevent their full maturity as Christians and persons.

This view of the Church and the world is reflected in several of the council documents. It is particularly evident in *Lumen Gentium's* treatment of the laity. The task of the laity is to bring the Gospel to the marketplace. The mission of the Church cannot be fulfilled by the clergy alone. Since that mission is to the world, the laity are particularly necessary. Their special task is to bring the life of the Church into the marketplace. Technology, culture, politics, economics and every other area of human life needs to be enlightened by the gospel and the life of the Church.

The Genesis command to subdue and transform the earth is carried out by Christians by their living of the Gospel in

[26]Vatican II. *Ad Gentes* #2.

their everyday lives. Thus all of creation (which "groans" for salvation) is daily sanctified through the grace of Jesus Christ at work in each Christian.

At the present time, the Holy Father, John Paul II, and the Roman Curia are adamant that the clergy should not become involved in politics. There is a great deal to be said for this stance against partisan politics. It is important for the Church to carry on its own mission in this area. At times Church and State must be in confrontation. Too close an alliance between the clergy and government may not be in the best interest of either.

For this reason it is imperative that the laity take an active part in politics. This is especially true in democracies because there government *is* the people. Not to be involved is simply to shirk one's duty as a citizen. The danger of such neglect is government and decision by default.

Similarly in the world of economics, the laity are naturally involved. The Church is a non-profit organization. It is not the Church's task to make money, to provide jobs or to be responsible for economic development. Clergymen are not readily a part of the economic scene, except perhaps as a reminder that conscience needs to be a part of economic decisions. But the laity are called upon by their very secularity to be a part of the world of economics.

Cultural development in all of its aspects: the arts, communication, education, environment, etc., are all areas where the laity serve God and neighbor. Building a sound mind and sound body, providing recreation and sensitivity to spiritual values in life are all important to human development. And the laity exercise their vocation and become holy in the pursuit of these ends.

Transforming the world and building the city of God in the city of man is clearly where the laity carry on the mission of the Church. The clergy are called to serve the Church and minister to its spiritual needs. The clergy are also part of the Church and the world. In many ways they remain part of the laity, God's people, except in the measure that their call requires a separation from the laity. This integration of the clergy into the *laos* has been achieved to a much greater extent in the Protestant clergy. It is also an integration that can be seen in the Orthodox communion. Whether or not Rome will maintain its present segregation as it becomes more the "world church" that Rahner envisioned remains to be seen. In all probability some of the "integration" will rub off. But whatever may become of the clergy, the laity will assume an ever greater role in the mission of the Church. That role will above all be concerned with the task of the Church in the world.

But Vatican II has also indicated that the role of the laity is not only in the world. It is also in worship. The altar rail has been removed, symbolic of the separation of the clergy and laity. We have not drawn fully the implications of that gesture. But already the laity feel quite at home in the sanctuary. They have become our readers, leaders of song, servers, ministers of Communion. The Council has clearly understood that the liturgy (*laitos ergon*) is the people's action/work. It should never have been, and never should be something exclusively clerical.

By virtue of their Baptism, every person in the Church shares in the priesthood of Jesus, and has a right and obligation to offer "spiritual sacrifices" to the Lord (1 Pet 2:5). Sharing in the self-offering of Christ, the laity rightly offer their own selves and their lives along with the once-for-all sacrifice of Jesus, the Son of God. Ordained priesthood orders this celebration. Priests are trained and ordained to offer the sacrifice fittingly, and to lead the people in worship. But the worship does not belong to anyone except the entire people of God and Christ their high priest.

The Eucharist and the Laity

No less than for the clergy, the Eucharist must be the center of the life of the laity. As Schillebeeckx described it, the Eucharist is the ebb and tide of the Christian's life.[27] The Council has described it as the summit and source of the Christian life and apostolate. Thus the laity bring all of life—their human life—to the Eucharist and offer it to God with Christ's self-offering. They receive from the Eucharist the divine life (grace) which makes it possible for them to grow as Christians into the mature "Christ come to full stature."

Their communion with Christ developed through Scripture and the life of prayerful contemplation insure that the spirit will guide them as they seek to apply the Gospel to a never-ending series of changing and developing situations throughout their Christian lives.

But the Eucharist is not some kind of magic moment. It must be a genuine celebration, proclamation and communion. For this reason clergy and liturgy planners must look to the quality and inspiration potential of the celebration rather than the availability (filling-station mentality) of "Masses." The liturgical rule is for a single, fully developed liturgy for each congregation.[28] Only pastoral necessity should add to that number. Such a celebration should make it possible for sharing and full participation on the part of all. Lectors, leaders of song, servers, eucharistic ministers are needed. Communion with real-life bread and sharing of the cup becomes possible in such a setting. Music, the arts, homily are also possible when the celebration is scheduled at a time convenient for all—and for genuine *celebration*.

The shortage of priest-celebrants is often used as an excuse for slipshod liturgy. Would it not be more convenient and appropriate to use permanent deacons and lay leaders in genuine liturgy than celebrants who are exhausted by an overbearing schedule? Aren't clergy trying to prove they are needed rather than working to empower the laity so that they are really not indispensable?

[27]Edward Schillebeeckx. *Christ the Sacrament of the Encounter With God.* Tr. by Paul Barrett. English text rev. by Mark Schoof and Lawrence Bright. N.Y. Sheed and Ward, 1963.

[28]*Eucharisticum Mysterium* (Instruction on the Worship of the Eucharistic Mystery, 25 May, 1967) #26.

Once we have begun to truly understand how all the pieces fit together in the Church, perhaps we will then begin to understand how the Church can truly serve and transform the world. The Eucharist is the sign of the Church. When it truly reflects our understanding of Church as described in *Lumen Gentium* then it will truly be "Bread for the life of the world."

The Laity and the Future of the Church

We are not looking into a crystal ball to predict the future. Rather we are reading the signs of the times and asking the Spirit to help us discern direction and guidance for the future. "The writing is already on the wall." The shortage of vocations is directly proportionate to the growing awareness of the role of the laity in the Church. The laity are the answer to the shortage of vocations, and the shortage is not a disaster. It is an opportunity to develop other ministries in the Church: permanent diaconate, eucharistic ministers and other lay ministries, reorganization of chanceries and parish responsibilities.

While much of this trend is new in the western Roman Catholic polity, it is part and parcel of ordinary life in other communions. We seek to reverse the clericalism of the twelfth century and afterwards. The reformers lamented that development in the Church and tried to eliminate it. We can learn from the experience of our Protestant and other Christian brothers and sisters in this regard.

Vatican II has placed all of this *"aggiornamento"* not on a practical basis, but on a theological one. It is appropriate that the laity be given their rightful place in the Church. Whether we have an abundance of clergy or not, it will still be appropriate for the laity to keep the place given them in *Lumen Gentium* and other documents of the Council.

The full picture of what the Church will look like when the laity fully *emerge* is not clear. The role of women both in religious life and in secular calling deserves special consideration. We have just begun to ask ourselves what their place ought to be. Paul VI's statement about women's ordination[29] does reflect the past and what is normative at the present time. It does not lock the door for the future. Ecumenical sensitivity requires openness to *all sides* of the issue. The American experience of the role of women in society is far different from that experience elsewhere, even in Western Europe. The question needs to be open for a long time yet before a final decision is possible.

Ecumenical Implications

The developing spirituality of the laity has tremendous importance for Church unity. While Orthodox and Roman Catholic polity has been extensively clerical, Anglican, Lutheran and Protestant polity has been very open to lay participation at all levels. Sharing this experience is yet another way for ecumenism to be practiced and bear fruit for Christian living.

In terms of the eventual reunion of Christendom, developing lay spirituality is vital to the ecumenical venture. Whether we think in terms of a "communion of communions"[30] (which seems more useful at this time) or in terms of corporate reunion (which seems to be envisioned in "sister-Church" and other bi-lateral concepts), the view of the Church on laity is crucial. We cannot continue to act according to pre-Vatican patterns and clerical attitudes, and expect that Christian unity will move forward.

Lay participation in bi-lateral dialogues is required by the very nature of the composition and polity of other churches. For a genuine meeting of equals, the laity must continue to "emerge" in all Christian Churches.

[29]Paul VI, Pope "Declaration on the Question of the Admission of Women to the Ministerial Priesthood" SCDF *Origins* 6 (1977) 517-524.

[30]Cf. J. Robert Wright. *A Communion of Communions.*

Particularly in Rome's effort to treat the Anglican Communion as a "sister-Church"[31] and move toward corporate/ visible unity, the role of the laity is crucial. A complete disparity of attitudes would negate convergence.

ARCIC I in its *Final Report* suggested that women's ordination should not be church-dividing.[32] It is a very moot question in both churches. Whatever the determination of each of the churches, women's role in the Church and the development of ministries will continue to be very important.

The development of lay ministries of all kinds is occurring in all of the churches. It is useful that they be expanded ecumenically, i.e., with consultation of other churches, and with the advantage of their experience.

Spiritual theology and ministerial programs are developing across church lines. In some places deacon programs are being conducted jointly. Programs for spiritual growth, marriage preparation, confirmation, retreats, etc., are being conducted with a realization that there is so much in common that pooling resources is to the advantage of all.

The task and mission of the Church to the world is service and witness; the Churches would do well to join in this witness and service. The Churches must make the most of their limited resources. The laity continues to be a neglected resource in virtually all churches to some degree. Mobilizing this resource is another avenue of ecumenical cooperation and moving toward greater Church unity.

[31]See Robert Hale. *Canterbury and Rome: Sister Churches.* A Roman Catholic Monk Reflects upon Reunion in Diversity, London, Darton-Longman-Todd, 1982. x, 188p. esp. p. 105-144.

[32]ARCIC I. *The Final Report.* Elucidation (1979) #5.

2

Communion with Christ

One of the great rediscoveries of our day is communion (koinonia). It is easy to think of the Christian life as something rather extrinsic to the individual. A nod to the catechism, an acceptance of a creed. Communion suggests a union of lives and an inner dynamism which is a way of life and a deep relationship best described as friendship or intimacy. The lives of the saints reflect this kind of relationship and way of life. St. Paul frequently describes the Christian as living "in Christ." He states "it is no longer I who live, it is Christ who lives in me" (Gal 2:20).

Grounded in Faith

Communion with Christ begins with faith. Faith is God's invitation to communion and the Christian's acceptance. Operating and cooperating grace are involved. Faith is thus God's gift. Abraham is praised for his faith because "Abraham believed and it was credited to him as justice."[1]

[1] Romans 4:3 quoting Genesis 15:6 and explaining it.

Faith is God extending his hand in friendship and the believer receiving it. Christ opens his arms in the embrace of friendship and the Christian embraces Jesus as Lord and Savior and Friend. Friends share their lives together. There is an overlapping of one life into the other. What is done for the friend is done for oneself, since the friend is another self. Friendships transform human beings and make them grow. Jesus is the incarnation of divinity and his life has power to make of us all children of God, brothers and sisters in the Lord, members of God's family by adoption and grace.

Faith is often discussed in connection with knowledge and revelation. Through faith we discover ever more and more about our friend Jesus. The initial act of faith, however justifying, is not the sum total of its activity in the Christian life. Like all the virtues it is destined to grow and to influence everyday activity. Being one of the cardinal theological virtues, and logically the first in the process of justification and sanctification, its influence is to be permanent and all-pervasive. It influences the measure of holiness a Christian possesses (if we consider holiness not simply in its essential element of charity, but in its wider reality of all the virtues). Our Christian life is grounded in faith.[2]

Faith is a fundamental option for God and Jesus Christ which the Christian makes. Every decision as a Christian is colored and affected by that fundamental and crucial option. Like the basic choice of life or death to sin.

As part of eucharistic spirituality faith is of vital importance. The Eucharist is the Sacrament of Faith in the sense that it challenges our faith constantly. Not only is faith challenged by the way in which Christ renews his Sacrifice or is present in the Eucharist. Faith is also challenged as a living reality. The Christian who celebrates the Eucharist and is united to Christ professes to believe in him and in his Gospel. Each Eucharist is related to the proclamation of the Gospel and shares in that proclamation. "Let us proclaim

[2]See "Faith" in *New Catholic Encyclopedia* v. 5 p. 792-804. N.Y. McGraw-Hill 1966.

the Mystery of Faith" the priest or deacon says after the words of Institution. And the congregation expresses and renews its faith with the response: "Christ has died, Christ is risen, Christ will come again."[3]

But the Eucharist must be a genuine sign of both God's gift and man's response. For this to be true, Christians must live what they proclaim, the death and rising of Jesus in their lives.

The Eucharist is both celebration and contemplation. Whether in the quiet moments of the Liturgy, after receiving the Lord, or in the quiet moments of prayerful reflection, the faith of the Christian is kindled, strengthened and renewed for Christian living. If faith has to do with light and revelation, such "eucharistic" moments reveal the risen Lord and his Spirit. Through Jesus we are united in deeper communion with the Father, Son and Spirit.

Communion In Trust

The Christian virtue of hope has two aspects.[4] The first has to do with the goal of the Christian life: eternal life with God in glory. The second has to do with reaching that goal, by trust in God's promise and will to save. While Christians often reflect on hope and its relationship to the goal of eternal life, perhaps they do not sufficiently make the most of hope as the exercise of trust. The rising rate of despair and suicide even among Christians can give us some idea of how the virtue of trust is not sufficiently part of the Christian make-up. Hope in terms of eternal goals may not have a great deal of motivating power at times. Hope as trust in the

[3]Roman Missal. Eucharistic Prayer 1- 4.

[4]"Espérance" *Dictionnarie de Spiritualité Catholique.* t. 4 Col.1208-1233. (Dictionnaire de Spiritualité: ascétique et mystiques, doctrine et histoire, fondé par M. Viller, F. Cavallera, J. de Guibert, S.J., . . . Paris, Beauchesne, 1957) "Hope" in *New Catholic Encyclopedia* vol. 7 p. 133-141.

Lord is crucial to survival as a Christian. Also the human dimensions of trust are readily understood. We cannot believe or love someone unless we trust them. The time and effort exerted in developing human trust can give us some idea of its importance in our relationship to Jesus and the Trinity.

Until recently, especially with Jürgen Moltmann's monumental "Theology of Hope,"[5] this virtue was fairly lost in medieval and sixteenth century controversy. Debate over the nature of the virtue became so confusing that Christians became discouraged from giving it any serious thought in practice. However, in a world of tensions, trust in God and hope for the future are very important. Spirituality today needs this virtue as an essential ingredient and orientation.

Eucharistic spirituality also needs hope. The Eucharist is the pledge of future resurrection and glory. Hope is intimately tied into communion in the Eucharist. Trust that God through the Eucharist, i.e., Jesus, the Bread of Life, will make the full banquet possible is ever related to the use of this Sacrament. "Christ has died, Christ is risen, Christ will come again" is our response to Christ's gift of himself and his Sacrifice. This hopeful response develops a hope-filled life and attitude.

In the Christian's trust there is a loving response to Christ's invitation: "trust me," "I can save you." There can be little doubt about Jesus' desire to save. But salvation is not possible without trust. Nor is love possible without it.

There is an indissoluble relationship between the theological virtues which is often forgotten. You cannot have one without the other. But it is precisely in the working relationship of the theological virtue that the Christian life is lived. We do not live in compartments. Life is an integrated reality. And so faith, and trust, and love all interact as we pursue God and allow him to pursue us.

---

[5]Jürgen Moltmann. *Theology of Hope*. N.Y. Harper and Row, 1957.

Trust, like faith, is not a once-for-all virtue. It is a developing relationship to God. As faith and charity grow, so does Christian hope. God leads us further and further into the darkness where alone we can truly "see" or know God. The mystics are clear. God is not to be found in the blaze of intellectual concepts, but in the night of loving contemplation. God is "felt" more than he is understood. He is tasted more than observed.[6]

In this context the Eucharist develops hope. In the splendor of liturgy we touch the beauty of God and contemplate his majesty. In the quiet of eucharistic contemplation we are drawn into the lovely night of his love. Nurtured by the Bread of Life, hope and trust grow to the point where faith and love can reveal God more intimately. We can believe our friend because we experience his love and salvation. In this atmosphere, however obscure, trust grows.

Lived in Love

The heart of spirituality is charity, as it is the essence of Christian holiness. The great commandment is love of God and neighbor. The essence of the Sermon on the Mount is that we become perfect in love as the Father is.

The Christian concept of "agape" is unique. The Old Testament command is to love God "with all your heart, all your mind, and all your will" (Deut 6:5). "Love your neighbor as you love yourself" is its parallel (Matt 22:39). But Christian love shares a divine quality. It is the human response to divine love. Friends are either equals or become equals. Human and divine love can become one in communion only if the human person is raised by God to a higher

[6]See St. John of the Cross. Ascent of Mount Carmel. *The Collected Works of St. John of the Cross.* Transl. by Kieran Kavanaugh, O.C.D., and Otilio Rodriquez, O.C.D. Washington, DC. ICS Publications, 1979. p. 192; also M. Ledrus, SJ. *Introductio in Doctrinam S. Joannis A Cruce: De Contemplatione.* Romae, P.U.G., 1955. p. 44-45.

level. This is the kind of love Paul describes when he states that the Holy Spirit is given to us so that we might love God in a divine way (Rom 8:14-17). This Spirit of Love first helps us to understand that by grace we become God's children, part of his family. Because we are children by grace and adoption, we can return our Father's love. Indeed it is the Spirit who loves the Father in us, and whose love we make our own. The Son's love is also something we share, as his brothers and sisters. And we love the Father "in and with" Christ.

Christian love is therefore a gift. Poured out by the Father and the Son, it is the gift of the Spirit and the gift of supernatural charity. But it also has its human side. We do not love God with our heads or hands. We love him with human hearts. This is not to say that Christian spirituality today is sentimentality. Nor is it to be entirely identified with charismatic enthusiasm. But Christian love must be real. This genuineness rests on the measure of genuine faith and trust we have. It also rests on the realization that charity is more God's gift than our action. Charity is poured into our hearts by the Spirit, God's great gift. As we contemplate this gift in our hearts, we begin to know and experience God's love. We are "compelled" to love God because we know his love (2 Cor 5:14).

Christian love also has to do with love of neighbor. John tells us it is the only test of the authenticity of our love. If we do not love the neighbor whom we can see, how can we be sure we love God whom we never see. (1 Jn 4:20). What we do to others, especially the least, will be the standard of eternal judgment. If we love Christ the head, we must also love the members of his Body.

The Eucharist is communion with Christ and with all the members of his Body. It is the Sacrament by which we taste the sweetness of the Lord and his loving friendship. Love is communion: the union of lives into one. Through the Eucharist our communion with Christ and our neighbor grow. United to Christ we cannot help but be united to the members of Christ's Body.

This union with Christ is in faith, hope and love. Christ our friend invites us into a deeper self-revelation, a relationship of trust and a growing union of lives. To be a Christian, then, is to live with Christ, "in Christ." This is a dynamic relationship, as all living and loving friendships should be. We experience the agony of Christ's cross and the ecstasy of his resurrection. The Eucharist is the high point of this experience of the mystery of Christ. We celebrate his death and rejoice in his resurrection. We look forward to his coming in glory when the mirror-like contemplation in the night of faith will give way to the full daylight of glory. With Christ we experience the joy of living and the drag of human limitation.[7] We work for the kingdom and realize that our struggle is not with flesh and blood but with the superpowers of enlightened darkness. Principalities and powers hold the world captive in sin. The measure of our progress is in proportion to the power of Christ's grace over their evil strength. With Christ we work for human rights, world peace, justice and equality in sharing the burdens of human life. We work for unity and the elimination of prejudice racial, religious, ethnic and sexist. With Christ, our friend, we seek to develop love and understanding, compassion and empathy, friendship and human sharing.

Our union with Christ is celebrated in Liturgy, deepened in prayer and lived in the daily struggle of the marketplace. If life is real, so is our love of Christ. The Eucharist is a celebration of daily life and constant love.

Communion with the Trinity

Communion with Christ is more than a human relationship. He is the Son of God, the Word. He reveals the Father through his Gospel, but also in the intimacy of a family relationship. As God's Son he can speak to us of the Father and help us to understand the Father's love and desire to

[7]See Teilhard de Chardin. *The Divine Milieu.* p. 45–68.

save. He can give the Spirit and through the Spirit make us
realize more deeply that we are God's children.

Though the Old Testament has a few references to God as
Father (and Mother), still it was Jesus Christ who fully
revealed God as Father. One who cares for lilies and birds is
surely one who can love and care for us. The Father's creative genius and fatherly care are proverbial and can be wit-
nessed everywhere. Natural disasters identified as "acts of
God" are perhaps so many exceptions to the marvelous
harmony of nature and the tangible proof of God's love and
providence. The exception confirms the rule. The disaster
does not negate God's continuing care.

The Father's mercy is the flip side of his love. Love cannot
exist without forgiveness. Neither can God's. No one has
spoken of God's mercy in such loving terms as Jesus. The
stories of the prodigal son and the lost sheep indicate how
much God desires to forgive. His forgiveness, unlike our
own, is not based on merit but on infinite love.

The Father is one who loves and gives. God, our Father,
so loved the world, he gave his Son for its redemption. He
continues to give his Spirit to make us holy and children
more like him in love.

Father and children are correlative. We are God's children
by adoption (we cannot be more fully his children than by
grace) and he loves us. Returning his love is another way of
describing Christian spirituality. Even the Eucharist relates
to the Father and his love. When we dine with Christ it is at
the Father's table, our songs of praise and thanks are
directed to the Father. The Sacrifice Christ offers is one of
praise and thanksgiving for all the marvels (*mirabilia Dei*)
wrought by the Father from creation to the parousia. Prin-
cipally we thank the Father for the mystery of Christ, his
coming in the Incarnation, his suffering and death by which
we are saved, and his resurrection and glorification. Christ's
eternal prayer of intercession becomes our own through the
Eucharist. And the Risen Lord gives us again his Spirit as
the Father's own gift.

With Christ we beg forgiveness and daily bread, especially

the bread of grace and divine life. We pray for the world's needs and our own.

In the Spirit

The Eucharist is communion in the Spirit. Just as the theological virtues are inseparable, so also are our relations to the Trinity. Communion with the Son and Father involves us particularly in a relationship with the Spirit. That relationship needs to be explored at length. For now suffice it to say that the Spirit is crucial to the development of grace, the virtues and our relationship to the Trinity. The Spirit helps us to understand the Father's love and our filiation. The Spirit loves in us and we must be attuned to this love. The Spirit transforms the bread and wine into the Body and Blood of Christ and transforms all Christians into the Mystical Body of Christ.

The Christian life is fundamentally an interpersonal relationship. We relate to Jesus Christ as our Savior, and through him to Father and Spirit. We are the Father's children and are born through and in the Spirit. Our sharing in the mission of Jesus is fulfilled through the inspiration and grace of the Holy Spirit.

After instituting the Eucharist Jesus was able to say: "I no longer call you servants but friends" (Jn 15:15). His life was at an end, his mission was completed, his sacrifice was immanent, salvation was at hand. He had revealed the Father, preached the Gospel, given proof of his divinity. Soon he would say: "it is finished." Now he could call his disciples "friends." He had given them all he had except his life, and that was already given in principle in the Eucharist. If Jesus statement "greater love no one has. . ." (Jn 15:13), is true, then he could surely now say "friends." The reason Jesus gives is "because I have revealed the Father to you" (Jn 15:15); and indeed he had. The gift of the Spirit simply enhances the disciples' understanding of this revelation.

Self-revelation and the revelation of one's interpersonal

relationships are an important part of friendship. The continual revelation of one's insights into the "passing parade" of life is an essential part of friendship's communication. Dante draws strength from Beatrice's eyes to see God in heaven.[8] God is also revealed in the insights of friends. The greatest insight of all was Jesus' vision of the Father. No one knows the Father except the Son and whomever the Son chooses to reveal him (Jn 1:18). Another text squarely placed in the context of the Eucharist.

The entire sixth chapter of John's Gospel is an explication of Jesus' statement on friendship. Through the Bread of Life, Jesus will give communion with the Father (and the Spirit). Eternal life is the result of both faith in Christ and communion in the Bread of Life. The flesh does not reveal the truth of this union. Only the spirit.

> "As I who am sent by the living Father, myself draw life from the Father, so whoever eats me will draw life from me...anyone who eats this bread will live forever" (Jn 6:57-58).

And so communion with Christ leads to communion with the Father, Spirit and the Body of Christ. It is all a matter of friendship. Love and friendship lead to one life and caring and sharing for one another. The love we have for God began with God and continues on God's initiative.

Union with Christ in Liturgy

The centrality of the Eucharist in the Christian life is clear to everyone after Vatican II. However there is a lingering malaise due to a lot of tridentine theology that hovers over our people. Having been raised in an atmoshpere of *"ex*

---

[8]Dante Alighieri. *The Divine Comedy. Hell, Purgatory, Paradise.* Tr. by Henry F. Cary. With introduction and notes. New York, Collier 1909. (Harvard Classics 20). Paradiso. Canto xxx.

opere operato," understood as the Sacraments operate automatically, it is difficult for many to achieve the proper balance in their spirituality between the action of Christ and their personal efforts and cooperation. The Council of Trent did not say the Sacraments operate automatically. Repeating Thomas Aquinas, the Council emphasized that the essential power of the Sacraments is not dependent upon the faith or devotion of the minister. Their efficacy was rather dependent upon the action of Christ *(ex opere operantis Christi)*.[9] At the same time (though forgotten in the postconciliar dust of controversy), the Council emphasized that the cooperation of the recipient was not unimportant *(ex operantis)*.[10]

However it took the liturgical movement and the Second Vatican Council to bring the two into proper focus. Both the action of Christ and the cooperation of all other agents (especially the recipient) are important. The minister, the choir, the artist, the assembly, the lectors and communion distributors all have a role to play if liturgy is to be effective in the lives of Christians.

In this context we might consider union with Christ through the Eucharist. For genuine union it is not sufficient for the communicant simply to "receive the host." While Christ is presumed to give grace if the recipient poses no obstacle *(non ponentibus obicem)*,[11] still we are talking of minimal fruit from the Sacrament. Unfortunately that was

[9]St. Thomas Aquinas. *Summa Theologiae*—Latin Text and English translation. Blackfriars ed. N.Y. McGraw-Hill 1975. vol. 66 III Q. 64 a. 3 & 4. See also Council of Trent. Session VII can. 8. Denz. #851. which simply uses "ex operato" thus: If anyone shall say that by the said sacraments of the New Law, grace is not conferred from the work which has been worked (ex opere operato), but that faith alone in the divine province suffices to obtain grace: let him be anathema. (Denz. #851) Deferrari transl.)

[10]Council of Trent. Session XIII. Cap. 7 & 8 Denz #880, 881, 882.

[11]"non ponentibus obicem" Council of Trent Session VII Can. 6 Denz #849.

the ground of controversy in the sixteenth century. (Perhaps the reformers were more concerned with fruitfulness than with "validity" as we understand it today.) Rather than a minimalist view of Sacraments and the Christian life, we think today much more in maximalist terms. How can we get the most out of what we are doing as Christians? (Otherwise, why bother?) Union with Christ is more than something extrinisic, passing or unengaging. To be united to Christ is to live differently. This is really what the Christian seeks through the Eucharist.

In this context we see the importance of a eucharistic spirituality, i.e., an integration of the Eucharist into our Christian living. The liturgical celebration in this context is the crowning point of the ebb and tide of life. We come to the Liturgy to hear God's word in its primordial setting and to engraft it into our lives. We proclaim the word and celebrate the Mystery of Christ which fulfilled it in human history. We share in the mystery and are saved by the action of Christ who touches our lives with healing and grace. We are caught up in the transformation of the Resurrection and are given the Spirit.

In moments of contemplation we reflect on what we receive and deepen our openness to grace. We clarify the direction of our life and how we might implement what we hear in God's word and what we receive through his Sacrament. More particularly, our union with Christ has grown. We hear again his word of friendship and experience the warmth of his love. He wants to save us, and through us he wants to touch other lives with salvation.

Our prayer and our Christian asceticism open the way to God's grace (and yet even cooperating grace is God's gift). We are not passive recipients of divine life. Eternal life grows and is lived in a vibrant, free and living person. Persons grow or decline. Our union with Christ intensifies.

Asceticism is the purification of love, as prayer is its intensification. There should be nothing masochistic about Christian asceticism. For love to be pure, many impurities must be removed. Selfishness, pride, lust, greed are so many obstacles to love. And the greatest of these is selfishness. St. Peter Julian Eymard placed at the center of eucharistic spirituality the *gift of self*.[12] As Carl Truhlar, S.J. points out in his now famous "*Antinomies*,"[13] this gift of self or abnegation, is the other side of love. Not only is it death to self-love, but it is also a positive desire to give oneself to God, the radical gift of one's self to God to serve his people and his reign.

Only a gift of this kind can adequately match the gift Christ makes of himself in the Eucharist. Perhaps this explains why Jesus prophesied his fulfilling of the Father's will on the cross and gave the call to abnegation in the same breath:

> "If a man wishes to come after me, he must deny his very self, take up his cross and begin to follow in my footsteps" (Matt 16:24).

Having made the radical gift of oneself to Christ, and renewing it daily with the eucharistic memorial of Christ's cross (and our own), the Christian then pursues the mission of Jesus, walking in his footsteps. The strength for this journey through life comes from the Bread of Life, the source of life "from the Father" and the cause of future resurrection.

We shall have more than one opportunity to speak of the work of prayer in deepening our union with Christ. Here we wish to draw attention to the source of that union in the Liturgy of the Eucharist. We have emphasized the need for genuine celebration because the grace of God is not impervious to it. We would like to emphasize it from the point of view of the recipient, the person in the pews. Whether or not the Liturgy is inspiring, celebrated in an atmosphere of calm, prayerful union with Christ is truly important. The communicants can "supply" their own devotion. People have been doing it for centuries. But the Vatican Council helps us

---

[12]Cf. Nunez. La Spiritualité. . . p. 310-330.

[13]Carl Truhlar, SJ. *Antinomiae Vitae Spiritualis*. Rome, 1958. Ch. 5. Conscientia Proprii Valoris et Humilitatis. p. 153-245.

to understand that the normal way for people to be inspired is for the clergy and the assembly to be holy and united with Christ. Nothing can really substitute for such a dimension. If it is lacking God can provide, but not without some minor miracle of grace.

On the other hand, the recipient must bring his own soul to the celebration. Attention, devotion, reverence are all important. Preparation to hear and understand the word of God and to share deeply in the Sacrament are also of extreme importance. There are no spectators at Liturgy, only participants. The Liturgy by definition is "the people's action." Their active, intelligent and vibrant participation is essential to the fruitfulness of the Eucharist. All who are involved in the celebration must understand how they contribute to the total grace received. Intelligent reading, prayerful singing, external decor—all contribute to make the mood for grace-filled celebration.

The Eucharistic Banquet, like any meal, needs to be prepared and tasted. It cannot be rushed. It cannot be celebrated haphazardly or casually. After all, it is the Liturgy of the Lord.

Proclamation, source of liberation and communion, the Liturgy is the high moment of the Christian's day and the source of union with Jesus and the Trinity. Mainspring and wellspring of the Christian life and mission, the Eucharist empowers the Christian to establish God's reign in the city of men and women.

3

One in Christ's Body

Christians readily understand that the Eucharist is the greatest source of communion with God through Christ.[1] Our innate desire to know, love and serve God is satisfied and grows through the Eucharist. Our intimate knowledge of Christ as friend increases as we sup with him at the Lord's table and experience the reality of our belonging to the family of God.

The logical link between love of God and love of neighbor is also clear. But it is not always realized in its final consequences or implemented by Christians in their daily lives. The individualism which religion exemplified even for centuries is part of the cause of our separating our relationship to God and our relationship to neighbor. It takes prayer, reflection and asceticism to incorporate the two great commandments into our personal lives.

The doctrine of the Mystical Body of Christ is helpful to us for such integration. This doctrine stresses that we are not united to Christ in isolation, but as a member of Christ's

[1]Robert Kress. *The Church: Communion, Sacrament, Communication.* New York, Paulist 1985. esp. p. 30-107.

Body. Christ loves every member of his Body, as we love every member of our own. Each is an integral and important part of the whole. One does not love the body and hate the eye, the ear or the hand. One loves both head and feet, arms and legs. And so it is with Christ.

The Synoptics

While the Synoptic Gospels do not contain a theology of the Mystical Body, they do stress the intimate connection between love of God and love of neighbor. When Jesus is asked what is the great (or greatest) commandment he answers it is love of God "with all your mind, all your heart, all your will." He hastens to add: "And the second (commandment) is like it: you shall love your neighbor as yourself." (Mt 22:36-40). Love of neighbor is the hallmark of the Christian.

The final judgment will be an examination of our lives from a single point of view: whatever we did to the least of our brothers and sisters, we did to Christ.

The second commandment is *like* the first because it has to do with love. Love of neighbor is a test of our love for God because it is the concrete implementation of God's commandment. "If you love me, keep my commandments" (Jn 14:21).

In this context John's Gospel adds: "Love one another *as I have loved you*" (Jn 13:34). He calls this the *new* commandment. Not new in its essence, but new in its measure and its model.

The Synoptics stress that we are to love our neighbor because this is the practical way of being like the Father who is even-handed in his love: "Be ye perfect (in love) as your heavenly Father is perfect" (Mt 5:48).

John's Theology

Repeating and amplifying what the Synoptics say about love and neighbor, John develops the reasons why love of neighbor is so important. If we say we love God but do not love our neighbor, we are not telling the truth. For how can we love God whom we do not see, if we do not love the neighbor who is very visible. In John's epistle love of neighbor is clearly the touchstone and proof of our love of God (cf. 1 Jn 4:20-21).

Vine and Branches

John begins to uncover the doctrine of the Mystical Body in his fifteenth chapter. There he uses the example of vine and branches. Jesus is the vine, we are the branches. Isaiah had already spoken of God as the vinedresser and his people as the vine (cf. Is 5:1-7). The love and care of God for his people underlies John's theology. But the union between Jesus and the Christian is more intimate. We are grafted into the very life of Jesus Christ. The Father, as in Isaiah's example, trims the branches for fruitfulness, but the source of life is the vine, Jesus.

In his sixth chapter John relates growth in eternal and divine life with the Eucharist. In the fifteenth chapter there is a hint at the same reality: just as the branches cannot live without clinging to the vine, so neither can we have life or fruitfulness without Christ.

John's Sixth Chapter

An entire book could be written about John's sixth chapter[2] and its eucharistic theology. St. Peter Julian Eymard

---

[2]Raymond E. Brown, S.S. *The Gospel of John.* Anchor Bible vols. 29 and 29A Garden City, N.Y. Doubleday 1964.

carried this chapter over his heart and meditated it frequently.[3]
It speaks of the impossibility of eternal life without faith in Jesus. John then develops the idea that faith leads to communion with Christ as the Bread of Life.

> I am the bread of life... Anyone who eats this bread will live forever; and the bread that I shall give is my flesh, for the life of the world... Anyone who does eat my flesh and drink my blood has eternal life, and I shall raise him up on the last day. For my flesh is real food and my blood is real drink. He who eats my flesh and drinks my blood lives in me and I live in him.
>
> As I, who am sent by the living Father, myself draw life from the Father, so whoever eats me will draw life from me.
>
> This is the bread come down from heaven; not like the bread our ancestors ate; they are dead, but anyone who eats this bread will live for ever (Jn 6:48-58).

Communion with Christ reaches its greatest human expression in the Eucharist. The father's life is poured out through the Spirit who is given and from the life which flows from the Sacrifice of Christ on the cross. The risen life of the Lord, which is eternal, is transfused into the Christian by a deep loving faith and union with Christ, the Bread of Life.

If John speaks of Baptism as a *sine qua non* for eternal life in his third chapter, he completes that statement in the sixth chapter by stating that eternal life must be sustained by the Eucharist.

John does not draw the conclusion of necessary love of neighbor as a challenge of the Eucharist either in his Gospel or in his Epistles. However the conclusion is implied. You cannot love God without loving the neighbor. As love for God grows, so must love of neighbor.

[3]Albert Tesniere, S.S.S. *Peter Julian Eymard, the Priest of the Eucharist.* Rev. ed. N.Y. Sentinel Press 1954.

Paul's Theology[4]

Paul is much more explicit about the relationship between love of neighbor and the Eucharist. If we reconstruct the context of the Pauline statements on Eucharist in First Corinthians, we readily understand there can be no real Eucharist without love of neighbor.

The obvious context for First Corinthians is the dissensions in the Corinthian community. Paul treats of the matter directly in the eleventh chapter. But he makes a statement in the tenth chapter that is very important. He says:

> The blessing-cup that we bless is a communion with the blood of Christ, and the bread that we break is a communion with the body of Christ. The fact that there is only one loaf means that, though there are many of us, we form a single body because we all have a share in this one loaf (1 Cor 10:16-18).

(Paul then stresses that sharing in sacrifice is communion with the object of the sacrifice. This is the justification for the statement).

Thus the Eucharist is the source not only of our union with Christ, but also of our union with the members of his Body. We are all one because the loaf—Christ—is one.

In the eleventh chapter Paul develops this theme. He explains how the Lord instituted the Eucharist on the night before he died, and how the Eucharist is a proclamation of the death (and rising) of the Lord until he comes. He warns: therefore anyone who eats and drinks unworthily "will be behaving unworthily towards the body and blood of the Lord" (1 Cor 11:27). Many see all of this warning as relating to due reverence for the Eucharist. In reality it is a warning about the desecration of the Eucharist when love of neighbor is wanting.

[4]See Commentaries on *1 Corinthians*. Commentaries on *Ephesians*.

> Everyone is to recollect himself before eating the bread and drinking the cup; because a person who eats and drinks without recognizing the Body is eating and drinking his own condemnation. . .
>
> So to sum up, my dear brothers, when you meet for the Meal, wait for one another. Anyone who is hungry should eat at home, and then your meeting will not bring your condemnation. . . (1 Cor 11:28-34).

Many believe Jerome's addition of the word *"Lord"* to Body *(non dijudicans corpus Domini)* may have skewed the interpretation in the sense of appropriate preparation for Communion. But the text and context clearly emphasize that what Paul is condemning is a failure to recognize the needs of the neighbor and creating a countersign by the celebration of "the Meal."

This becomes even more evident as we add the dissertation on the Body of Christ of chapter twelve of First Corinthians and Paul's ode to charity in chapter thirteen. Clearly love of neighbor is not accidental to the Christian life and its central symbol, the Eucharist.

Paul explains in the twelfth chapter that the Spirit is the origin of the many gifts and charisms in the Church. He then says:

> Just as a human body, though it is made up of many parts, is a single unit because all these parts, though many, make one body, so it is with Christ. In the one Spirit we were all baptised, Jews as well as Greeks, slaves as well as citizens, and one Spirit was given to us all to drink (1 Cor 12:12-13).

Paul then explains how each part of the body is necessary. It is not possible for one part to say to another "I don't need you." We all need each other. All share both the joy and sorrow of sickness or health. Paul concludes:

> Now you together are Christ's body; but each of you is a different part of it. In the Church God has given the first place to apostles, the second to prophets, the third to

teachers; after them, miracles, and after them the gift of healing, helpers, good leaders, those with many languages... (1 Cor 12:27-28)

In his exhortation to the Ephesians, Paul plays on the same theme, encouraging his fellow Christians to preserve the unity of the Body of Christ:

> I, the prisoner in the Lord, implore you therefore to lead a life worthy of your vocation. Bear with one another charitably, in complete selflessness, gentleness and patience. Do all you can to preserve the unity of the spirit by the peace that binds you together. There is one Body, one Spirit, just as you were called into one and the same hope when you were called. There is one Lord, one faith, one baptism, and one God who is Father of all, over all, through all and within all (Eph 4:1-6).

Repeating the various gifts which the Spirit gives to make up the Body of Christ, Paul continues:

> ...so that the saints together make a unity in the work of service, building up the body of Christ. In this way we are all to come to unity in our faith and in our knowledge of the Son of God, until we become the perfect Man, fully mature with the fullness of Christ himself (Eph 4:12-13).

Communion with Christ involves union in love with our neighbor. Oneness in the Body of Christ leads to a unity of faith and service. You cannot love God, or Christ, without loving your neighbor.

In addition Paul links this love and unity in the body of Christ to the Eucharist. We desecrate the Eucharist without love of neighbor. The Eucharist is the full sign of Christ's love "to the end," given on the night before he died, broken as bread, symbolizing his brokenness on the Cross. To proclaim this death/resurrection without a living love behind it is to fail to discern the Body (of the Lord) in his Mystical Body, the Church.

Head and Members

The intimate union between the Head and the members of the Body of Christ is such that communion with the one entails union with the other. In this context we understand the Lord's injunction: "if you come to the altar and remember that your neighbor has anything against you, leave your sacrifice at the altar, and go and become reconciled with your neighbor. Then you can come and offer your sacrifice" (Mt 5:23-24).

Paul, in another passage, speaks of the love of Christ for the Church as the paradigm for human relations. He uses the example of the body. He says husband and wife should love each other as they love their own body. Paul then says that this symbol or mystery of love of husband for wife, Christ for the Church, has many implications. It is a deep mystery and the pattern of all human relations (cf. Eph 5:21-33).

The mission of Jesus, as described in Jn 11:52 is to reconcile the family of God's children. Unity among Christians is the beginning of the reconciliation of the entire human race. Salvation is both individual and collective. Jesus came to save you and me. He also came to form a people and a kingdom and to present that kingdom to the Father. We are not saved in isolation but as members of a Body. Our interdependence and interaction is vital to our growth in Christ and our individual salvation.

For many the work of Christian unity is not grasped as part of the Christian life. Working for unity by prayer or social action is seen as peripheral to the essence of being Christian. But you cannot separate love of God and neighbor. The social dimension of the Christian life is intimately united to its theological dimension. This fact explains why the Decree on Ecumenism states that growth in the Christian life is growth in spiritual ecumenism and vice versa. The Decree on the Church in the World makes it clear that the mission to the world of the Church is an essential and integral part of its mission of salvation.[5]

[5]See *Gaudium et Spes* #2 & 3.

Thus the Church is an instrument of the unity of all humanity. Bringing human dignity and human rights to all in the human family is important to bringing them salvation.

Ecumenical Implications

There are many implications and applications of the scriptural doctrine of the Eucharist as the sign and cause of the Mystical Body. The first implication is that faith and order, life and work are all intimately interconnected. If the Orthodox and Catholic communions are intent on faith and order according to other communions, the latter are seen as perhaps too committed to life and work. Orthodox and Catholics need to see the importance of life and work to the credibility of mission. Protestants and Evangelicals need to see faith and order as vital to the integrity and sincerity of social and ecumenical activity. There is a need for both groups to integrate both aspects as essential parts of a single whole. They are the two sides of the coin. Faith and action are the two wings that keep aloft and soaring the movement for unity.[6]

There will always be a tendency for one group to emphasize one aspect over the other. But in final analysis the mission of Christ and his Church to the world is the goal. Christian unity gives credibility to that mission. Unity in action helps us to appreciate unity in faith. Unity in faith emphasizes our action as the one activity of the Body of Christ.

The scandal of division deprives the action of the Body of Christ of its credibility. The hallmark of Christian authenticity is union in love *(koinonia).* The purpose of Christian community is service to the world. Building the kingdom requires the combined effort of everyone who believes in Christ. No member of the Body can be ignored or neglected. Everyone must pull their weight.

[6]See W.C.C., *Baptism, Eucharist, Ministry.* B#10 M#1-6.

And there is an urgency to the ecumenical agenda. Teilhard de Chardin said the parousia cannot take place until Christ's prayer is fulfilled and the Church has progressed to *point omega.*[7] Our unity cannot wait forever. Otherwise the Lord cannot and will not come. We need to make unity happen. This is the urgency underlying the entire ecumenical endeavor. The unity for which Jesus prayed is in his Body. The prayer is already fulfilled. The unity is a *given.* We profess in the Creed that the Church of Christ is one. What needs to happen is a recognition of that unity. The Vatican Council states:

> . . . it remains true that all who have been justified by faith in baptism are incorporated into Christ; they therefore have a right to be called Christians and with good reason are accepted as brothers (and sisters) by the children of the Catholic Church (UR#3).

While the Council also states that the unity we seek already exists in the Catholic Church, it recognizes the need for Catholics to work in the ecumenical movement for unity among all Christians. Yet there is a different point of view in Rome and Geneva. The World Council of Churches in its *Baptism, Eucharist and Ministry* stresses the theological reality of our incorporation into Christ by Baptism.[8] This reality far transcends our differences as Christians and Churches. The World Council sees the Catholic Church as another potential member. Rome insists on its uniqueness as the Church rooted in the Petrine and Pauline apostolic ministry.

We have obviously moved beyond the point where a "return to Rome" has any coinage or use as an ecumenical direction. Theologians must sublate a *"via media"* between the positions of Rome and Geneva to bring about the rap-

---

[7]Pierre Teilhard de Chardin. *The Phenomenon of Man.* N.Y. Harper, 1959. 318p. p. 257-264.

[8]W.C.C. *Baptism, Eucharist, Ministry.* B#6.

proachement needed at this time.[9] That middle road seems
to be grounded in a full recognition of the consequences of
incorporation into the Body of Christ. While visible and
institutional unity has its importance, such unity cannot be
achieved until (and after) the ontological reality of incorporation into Christ is fully recognized.

We are not integrated into Christ by halves. Either we are
members of the Body of Christ or we are not. Catholic
theology before the Council said that only Roman Catholics
were incorporated into the Body of Christ. The Council
came to realize that this position needed expansion. In the
Decree on Ecumenism the Church recognized Christian
Baptism in other Churches for what it is.

This is not to say that everyone gives the same mutual
recognition. Re-baptism has been condemned by WCC
BEM. Yet the practice continues. The reality of Christian
Baptism has not been accepted at the practical level.

This problem of baptismal recognition plagues other theological areas. In the Decree on Ecumenism the Church recognizes in principle that the Eucharist is *both* a sign of unity
achieved and a means of unity desired.[10] However the
Catholic Church has strictly limited the use of the Eucharist
as a means of unity. Other communions wonder why the
Catholic Church has done so. In their estimation valid Baptism is the key to licit reception of the other Sacraments.
While the New Code of Canon Law (#912) recognizes the
same principle, it does not fully follow through with its
consequences.

Without trying to resolve the many facets of this complex
problem here, we might simply point out the need for consis-
tency in the Roman Catholic position. On the one hand it
fully allows intercommunion with the Orthodox Churches
(that has been rejected by and large by the Orthodox) but
refuses, except in very limited circumstances "communion of

[9]Jeffrey Gros, F.S.C. *"Roman Catholic Identity and the
Ecumenical Challenge." Emmanuel,* vol. 90 p. 6-13. Jan. 1984.

[10]*Unitatis Redintegratio* #8.

hospitality" to validly baptized Anglicans, Lutherans and Protestants.

Communion of Hospitality

We accept in principle that intercommunion is reserved for that point in time when two Churches agree that sufficient common ground has been established to allow members of one Church to receive in another virtually at will. Such a state, according to the New Code of Canon Law, exists between the Roman Catholic Church and Eastern Churches, both those in communion with Rome and Orthodox.[11] (It is interesting that this position is officially taken both in the Vatican Council and in the New Code without any resolution of the Marian dogmas and the dogma of Papal Infallibility).

On the other hand Rome does not seem to be ready to afford a similar status to the Anglican and Lutheran communions even though at the level of theology and bilateral dialogue essential agreement has been reached on all church-dividing issues.

Our position is not "open communion" or even "intercommunion." We would urge as a first step eucharistic sharing, i.e. permission for validly baptized Christians whose faith in the Eucharist is the same as ours to be permitted to receive the Eucharist when pastoral and spiritual need suggests it. Such reception remains a personal choice, not a general invitation. Our reason for advocating such use of the Eucharist goes beyond mere pastoral (or humane) considerations. It touches the very heart of what the Eucharist is *by nature*, i.e., the Sacrament of Unity, the *nurture* of the Mystical Body of Christ.[12]

There was a time when our theology of Marriage considered that in an inter-church Marriage only one of the parties

[11]*Canon* #844. #2.
[12]See *Food For The Journey.* NADEO, 1985; esp. p. 35-38.

received a Sacrament. This theology simply falls apart in the light of Vatican II and current understanding of Sacraments. While the theology of inter-church Marriage needs development, we simply point to it as an indication of another example of what we are describing here.

The Eucharist is a sign of unity achieved. That unity will never be perfect even within a Church or Communion (Roman Catholic, Anglican, Lutheran, etc.). (One might note, for example, the Missouri Synod's unwillingness to have altar and pulpit fellowship with other Lutheran Synods in the U.S.A.) Perhaps it would be better to say the Eucharist is a means of unity desired. George Tavard, peritus at the Council who worked at the final wording of the Decree on Ecumenism on this precise point, indicates that the choice of the word *"indiscretim"* in the text was precisely to show that it is not a matter of either/or, but both/and. *Indiscretim* is regularly translated as "universally;" it should be translated "divisively," i.e., you cannot divide these two aspects of the Eucharist. When one receives the Eucharist or celebrates it, one is automatically both affirming the unity which the Church has achieved through the Eucharist and using it as a means of grace and further unity.[13]

In this context, then, communion of hospitality is simply making use of a good, pastoral occasion to affirm the unity which ontologically exists by reason of common Baptism in Christ, by which we are integrated into his Mystical Body. If we "fail to recognize the Body" as we celebrate Eucharist, we should be prepared to receive Paul's reproach to the Corinthians. The Eucharist becomes a countersign.

[13]George Tavard. *"Vatican II and Communicatio in Sacris"* (unpublished paper presented to ARC-USA December 11, 1984. N.Y. p. 17-18). Text available in *Food For The Journey* NADEO. 1985 p. 36.

4

The Eucharist and the Holy Spirit

The Holy Spirit is an important person. The Spirit is God, one of the three divine persons of the Trinity. It would be an exaggeration to say the Holy Spirit is a forgotten person. But the Holy Spirit is surely a neglected person.[1]

Western mysticism and Eastern liturgy have managed to stress our relationship to the Holy Spirit. The modern charismatic movement is recovering the importance of this divine person for an understanding of Scripture. Most Christians have some relationship to the Holy Spirit. But everyone can improve their relationship to the Holy Spirit.

St. Paul's theology of the Mystical Body of Christ is unintelligible without an understanding of the role of the Holy Spirit in uniting and unifying the Body of Christ. The work of the Holy Spirit in the Eucharist is also major in importance.[2]

[1] Yves Congar. *I Believe in the Holy Spirit.* New York and London, Seabury Press/G. Chapman, 1983.

[2] E. Falardeau, S.S.S. "The Eucharist as Invocation of the Spirit." *Pastoral Life* v. 33 p. 2-6 November 1984. And "Communion in the Spirit" *Emmanuel* v. 90 p. 567-68 and 573-74 December 1984.

These considerations and others help us to understand the importance of examining the role of the Holy Spirit in eucharistic spirituality today.

A. The Holy Spirit:
New Testament Insights

To understand the role of the Holy Spirit in the Christian life, we must first consider the Holy Spirit in the Trinity. Once we understand who the Holy Spirit is, we can better understand our relationship.

The Holy Spirit, we are told in the Scriptures, is the person who proceeds from the Father and the Son and is their mutual gift of love. Obviously that statement of faith is veiled in human and implicit terms. Gift, love, advocate begin to express the Holy Spirit's role in the Trinity and in our lives.

John 14—17

Some of our best information about the Holy Spirit is found in John's Gospel.[3] In the Lord's farewell discourse the Spirit is promised and described. The Spirit of Truth is sent by the Father and the Son to teach, to make clear what the Son has revealed, to witness to Jesus.

Because Christians better understand the teaching of Jesus they are gifted with God's peace (Jn 16:33). The unity of Christians is the gift of the Spirit. The Spirit directs Christians in the mission of the Church to the world. All this insight into the Spirit in John's Gospel is true because the Spirit is the Spirit of Truth, the Spirit of Love and Peace, the Spirit who witnesses to Jesus and his mission to the world.

[3]Raymond Brown, S.S. *The Gospel of John*. Anchor Bible vol. 29 and 29A.

Paul to the Romans, Chapter 8[4]

While John's Gospel speaks in general terms about the mission of the Holy Spirit, Paul is more specific about the work of the Spirit in the Christian life. In his Epistle to the Romans, chapter 8, Paul states that everyone moved by the Spirit is a child of God. (v.14). Being a child of the Father, or brother of Jesus, the Son, is a reality and lived out because of the grace and inspiration of the Spirit.

A very special area of the Spirit's influence is the area of prayer. The Spirit teaches us to pray (v.27). We pray badly. But the Spirit is always heard because he is the God of Love. He is intimately united to Father and Son; their loving expression. And so the Christian who prays "in the Spirit" knows not only to say "Abba" and "Jesus is Lord," but also to pray in quiet love, while the Spirit speaks in wordless "groans" and sighs of love.

The mystics make much of this non-verbal communication. Psychologists help us to understand its importance in human communication. We communicate a great deal more by our "body language" at times, than we do by our words. So it is with Christian prayer. What is in the heart is more important than what is on the lips. Isaiah complains about the people's prayer as being lip service without a heart (Is 29:13). The Christian's answer to that kind of prayer is prayer "in the Spirit." Prayer centered in the depths of the soul, attentive to the presence of the Spirit within, begins to reflect the pattern of the Lords' prayer: hallowed be thy name, thy kingdom come, thy will be done.

1 Corinthians, Chapter 12[5]

To fully appreciate what Paul has to say about the work of the Spirit in the Body of Christ, it would be good to recall

[4]Paul to the Romans, ch 8:1-27.
[5]1 Cor. 12:1-30.

the context of chapter 12 of his letter to the Corinthians. His *"object all sublime"* is to change attitudes in the community torn by divisions. If Christ came "to unite the scattered children of God" (Jn 11:52), divisions in the Christian community are intolerable and a scandal. Paul in chapter 10 and 11 of the First Epistle to the Corinthians stresses the compelling need for unity from the Eucharist and its primary effect of building one Body, the Body of Christ.

In this chapter Paul stresses the work of the Spirit toward the same end. In the Body of Christ every member is necessary. Indeed the weakest members of the human body are those most honored and revered. No member is useless or unnecessary. All contribute to the good of all. The Spirit distributed gifts and charisms to each member of the Body of Christ for the good of all (v.4-11).

> "Just as a human body, though it is made up of many parts, is a single unit because all these parts, though many, make one body, so it is with Christ. In the one Spirit we were all baptized...and one Spirit was given to us all to drink" (1 Cor 12:12-13)..."Now you together are Christ's body: but each of you is a different part of it" (ibid. v.27)

After this description of the Body of Christ and the work of the Spirit for its unity, Paul is prepared (in chapter 13) to encourage Christians to seek above all, not gifts and charisms, but charity which unites the Body of Christ in love.

The Spirit, God's gift of love, and the source of *agape* in the Christian heart, is poured out in Baptism and the Eucharist so that the Body of Christ may be built up in love. The Spirit is not only the bond in the Trinity, the Spirit is also the bond uniting the members of Christ's Mystical Body.

Thus the Church, the Body of Christ, is a *koinonia,* a communion. Not simply an institution or corporate body, the Church is a living reality. Divine and human, it is a communion between God and human persons, a loving relationship between Christians and between all men and women. The reformers were right in emphasizing that the Church was more the invisible reality of grace and communion, than the visible structure of a human society. But they were wrong in saying that the visibility of the Church was either non-existent or unimportant. Just as in the historical Christ there is a divine and human element, so is there a divine and a human element in the Mystical Body of Christ. The Word became flesh; his Church must also be incarnate in all who live the Christian life down the centuries.

Obviously what is more important to Christianity in the final analysis is not the health of the visible Church, but the spiritual life of the Mystical Body. Body and soul are important. The Vatican Council seeks a reform, a restoration and renewal of both.

B. *The Holy Spirit and the Eucharist*

We need to fix our reflections on the relationship between the Spirit and the Eucharist in the context of the Spirit's role in the Mystical Body. Popular piety and theology frequently see the Eucharist as a relationship between the Christian and Jesus. However, the Eucharist is the Risen Lord and his task is to be a "vivifying spirit." When the Lord appears to his disciples he often breathes upon them and says: "Receive the Holy Spirit" (Jn 20:22-23). So it is when the Risen Lord gives himself in the Eucharist.

The Eastern Churches are more atuned to the trinitarian dimensions of the Christian life and carry this perception into their theology of the Sacraments. Thus the epicletic dimensions of the Eucharist are more consciously in their theology. The new Roman Catholic Eucharistic Prayers in the Sacramentary exemplify a renewed awareness of the role of the Holy Spirit in the Eucharist. The Spirit transforms the elements of bread and wine into the Body of Christ. The same Spirit transforms men and women into the Mystical Body of Christ.

Louis Boyer treats this subject at length and develops with realism the role of the Holy Spirit.[6] He insists that the com-

---

[6]Louis Bouyer. *The Church of God.* Especially p. 252-264.

munion and communication between the Christian and the Trinity is not an ethereal and unrealistic idealism. The heart and soul of the Christian life is precisely our communion with God. This communion is simply not possible without the assistance of the Holy Spirit. In the Spirit God the Father gives himself and his love to us. We can return that love only in the same Spirit. Paul's theology of the Spirit makes the same theological point. We can only pray in the Spirit. Only in the Spirit can we confess that Jesus is Lord. Similarly we can say "Abba" (Father) only in the measure that the Spirit helps us to know we are God's children (cf. Rom 8:15-16).

Somehow in our understanding of the Eucharist we have failed to realize that the heart of the matter is *communion.* Not in the individualistic and pietistic sense of much post-reformation piety, but in the sense of profound biblical, patristic and theological truth. Post-Vatican II emphasis on the celebration as communitarian and participatory is a step in the right direction. What the Eucharist does is to build up the Body. It is not the thrill of the moment, being on Calvary symbolically, or being at the Supper. The Eucharist is the Risen Lord who gives us his Spirit to make of us the Body of Christ. The Spirit who hovered over the chaos in the original creation, now hovers over the Christian community to make it the Body of Christ.

At Communion we are not merely thrilled with a visit from Jesus. We are rather caught up in the dynamic love of Father, Son and Spirit. "As the Father has life, and I live because of the Father..." (Jn 6:57). The Eucharist is the outpouring of divine life because it is the gift of the Spirit who is the source of life. We receive Communion as the fruit of the Liturgy so that our Christian lives may be deepened by our response to divine love. The Spirit is given to us as energy so that we may keep the covenant and love God and neighbor. Without that gift in ever greater measure, it is impossible to move toward Christian maturity which is "Christ among you, your hope of glory" (Col 1:27).

The reason why reverence is so important to the eucharistic celebration is because it is the atmosphere of communion with God. We do not approach God casually. If we do, it is at the expense of love. Reverence is the sweet flower of love. It is part of the virtue of devotion which Thomas Aquinas stresses is so important to charity and worship. In our revision of the Liturgy, we have often tried to modernize at the expense of reverence. Such Liturgies produce little fruit if they do not help genuine *devotio* which unites *religio* and *caritas*.[7]

At the Communion of the Mass, then, we begin a communication with God at the personal level which is the foundation for our personal prayer throughout the day. Importantly, the new Liturgy calls for moments of silence after the distribution of the Eucharist. Such moments allow us to insert personal reverence and love. We pause to acknowledge and recognize the Spirit given to us by the Risen Lord.

This moment of quiet prayer and contemplation is the paradigm for eucharistic devotions of every kind. As the post-Vatican II decree on the subject implies, these devotions flow from the celebration and lead to it. They especially continue the prayer and communication which are at the heart of Communion itself.[7a]

The emphasis here is on contemplation, on the prayer of the Spirit rather than our own. Our prayer can only be human words. The Spirit prays in ineffable terms to God who is *the* ineffable. Our prayer is the prayer of Jesus, Risen Lord, who stands before God's throne forever (and in our hearts) and speaks to the Father on our behalf. In the presence of such prayer, silence is golden.

[7]St. Thomas Aquinas. *Summa Theologiae.* II-II q. 81-100, esp. q. 82. "Dévotion" DSC vol. 3 col. 702-716 and "Devotion" (Fondement Théologique) DSC vol. 3 col. 716-727. "Religion, Virtue Of" in *New Catholic Encyclopedia* vol. 12 p. 270-271 and 1979 update in vol. 17 p. 562.

[7a]S.C.D.W. *Eucharistiae Sacramentum* (on Holy Communion and the Worship of the Eucharistic Mystery Outside of Mass) 21 June, 1973. #80.

There is another dimension of Communion that is important. The relationship between the Risen Lord and the Spirit. The Risen Lord gives the Spirit. We may wonder why the Gospel makes this statement. The historical Jesus obviously had a special relationship to the Spirit. We see this clearly in the "good news" of the Annunication and in the Baptism of Jesus. However, the Resurrection makes Jesus pass into eternity. With his passover, Jesus becomes a "vivifying spirit." The Spirit of Jesus is now given to the Apostles and gives birth to the Church.

There is an intimate relationship between the Spirit and the Risen Lord. Humanity now has a very special instrument. The Second Adam replaces the first. Not only is human life within the power of the human race, but in Jesus is the power of giving the Spirit for the life of the world.

This intimate union between the Risen Jesus and the Spirit further explains the relationship between the Eucharist and the Spirit. The Eucharist is the efficacious symbol by which the Risen Lord gives his Spirit to us. And the reason the Spirit is given to us is so that we might have a deeper life and communion with the Father. John's sixth chapter clearly implies this dimension.

Thus the Eucharist is essentially trinitarian. It is not simply communion with Jesus. The purpose of our communion with Jesus is so that through him we can deepen our communion with the Trinity.

And so it is with eucharistic prayer. One of the great insights of St. Peter Julian Eymard was his perception of eucharistic prayer as related to Jesus, but through him to the Trinity.[8] In the final analysis we all search for God. We find him most intimately in the Eucharist because we are led to the Father by his Son in the Spirit.

The Spirit is also important to our relationship to the Risen Lord. The Gospels tell us that after the Spirit is given to the Christian community, it will come to understand in a

[8]Constitutions of the Congregation of the Blessed Sacrament #15.

new light and depth, the teachings of Jesus. Eucharistic prayer should make much use of the Scriptures. Many who center their lives around the Eucharist use the daily readings of the Liturgy as the basis for their eucharistic prayer. The role of the Spirit, given in Communion, given by the Risen Lord, is to clarify, explain, and give flesh to the Scriptures read. We assimilate God's word, we "put on Christ" as we contemplate the host of the Mass and the Spirit within us. God's self-revelation then becomes a personal revelation to us: "he loved me and gave himself up for me" (Gal 2:20). Such eucharistic contemplation has many dimensions. There is a word for the mind, there is love for the heart. There is an example for our life, there is the Spirit who unites us more deeply to the Risen Lord and thus with the Father, Son and Spirit.

Pondering the Gospel message in the light of the memorial *(anamnesis)* of the death, rising and glorification of Jesus, praying "in the Spirit" the Christian is thus prepared for his/her role to the world. The ultimate reason for Jesus' coming is to save the world from sin. The mission of the Christian is to enter into that salvific work. Building the Body of Christ is also building God's kingdom. That reign takes final shape in the Parousia. But it also must shape the world of today and tomorrow.

Teilhard de Chardin in a brilliant insight saw that the Spirit who hovers over the chaos in creation is the same Spirit who hovers over the world and its tranformation as Mass is celebrated over the earth.[9] St. Peter Julian Eymard used the slogan "Thy Kingdom Come" and paraphrased the statement by saying this kingdom would be built and would come through the Eucharist.[10]

Too often the Eucharist is perceived as personal piety without a relationship to the immediate world. A full understanding of the Eucharist includes a realization that the Eu-

[9]Pierre Teilhard de Chardin. *Hymn of the Universe.* N.Y. Harper and Row, 1965.

[10]Peter Julian Eymard. *Paraphrase of the Our Father.*

charist challenges the Christian to bring God's word and grace to the world. The gift of the Spirit is not for the Christian alone, but so that all may be instruments of transformation in the world. Jesus' injunction that we be light, salt, yeast for the world comes to mind. His mission was to unite into one the scattered children of God's family (Jn 11:52). Our mission is the same.

But the Eucharist is more than a memory of Christ's actions or a recalling of his words. It is the gift of the Spirit who energizes the Christian for the task of transforming the people and world around them into the Body of Christ and God's kingdom.

Thus the Eucharist touches every aspect of life: government and education, the arts and the sciences, industry and technology. Old and young, the well and the ill, the living and the dying—every facet of human life is affected by the Risen Lord and his Spirit.

C. Ecumenical Implications

This task of building the Body of Christ and transforming the world through the Spirit is not without its ecumenical implications. The Body of Christ in its visible expression as Church is divided. East and West, Protestant and Catholic are divided by centuries of prejudice and theological differences. Over 300 churches claim to be the visible and unique expression of the Body of Christ. Most of these churches have committed themselves to the ecumenical movement, the united effort to make the Church one.

The Catholic Church in the Vatican Council's Decree on Ecumenism has also endorsed the movement for unity. Its commitment is "irreversible."[11] Men and women who are baptized are brothers and sisters in the Lord and members of

[11]Pope John Paul II. Address to Roman Curia. June 29, 1985. (The Reality, Progress and Problems of Christian Unity). *Origins* v. 15 (1985) p. 125-128.

Christ's Mystical Body. The task of getting all to recognize this reality is part of the movement for unity.

For many people unity in the Church is a canonical matter. Once the Churches have sat down and worked out canonical differences and signed certain agreements, the Church will be one. For others the matter is theological. Once certain formulas have been agreed to or disclaimed, the Churches will be one. For those who have studied both the theology and the legal requirements of ecumenics and have some practical ecumenical experience the matter is much more one of *recognition* of what already exists rather than the creation of something new.

All who recite the Apostle's Creed profess that the Church *is* one. The unity of the Church is a *given*. The division of the Church is the scandal and the dilemma. How can the one Church have so many visible expressions? Obviously this is a matter of history and the misunderstandings that have divided the Church of Christ. Each of the churches claims to be the true Church of Christ. Some theories have stated that all of them are. Other theories claim that only one of these expressions is the true Church of Christ. Trying to achieve Christian unity by either of these approaches (and it has been tried many times) is probably doomed to failure. The World Council of Churches through its *Lima Document* on *Baptism Eucharist and Ministry*[12] has suggested another approach: that of mutual recognition. If the Churches can painstakingly and one-step-at-a-time recognize its baptisms, Eucharist and ministries as valid and genuine (by whatever process), it can then begin to move toward a common expression of apostolic faith together. Such recognition and confessions are seen as the first and most important steps toward unity in the Church of Christ. The outcome of this unity in terms of structure and ecclesiastical polity cannot yet be envisioned or described. Yet corporate unity is the ultimate goal. But the unity which can be achieved through mutual recognition and a common expression of faith is

[12]W.C.C. *B.E.M.* See esp. B.#15. E. #13 and M.#51-55.

sufficient to indicate to the unbelieving world that there is
one Church which has:

> ...one Body, one Spirit, just as you were all called into
> one and the same hope...There is one Lord, one faith,
> one baptism, and one God who is Father of all, through
> all and within all (Eph 4:4-6)

The way to such mutual recognition is through a realization that the Spirit binds those who are baptized into the
Risen Lord in a unity that far exceeds and excels Church
membership through registration. The life of the Father is
communicated through the Spirit by the Risen Lord and this
life and this Spirit are the deepest bond and reality that unify
Christians. History and human divisions cannot separate
what God unites in his divine way. Recognition of the realities which God creates in human hearts needs to transcend
the divisions of ecclesiastical polity and prescription. Canon
law needs to be written in the light of divine reality more
than for the preservation of ecclesiastical structures. This is
the "movement of the Spirit" and the "signs of the times."

The Eucharist is a sign of the unity which God desires.
Wherever the Supper of the Lord is real, the Spirit is given
to build the Body of Christ. George Tavard, ecumenist, suggests that the categories of *"valid/invalid"* used since the
Council of Trent are misleading.[13] They do not clearly reflect
the real situation they were coined to describe, nor the reality
of the present situation. Calling Anglican, Lutheran or Protestant Eucharists "invalid" because they do not meet canonical requirements of *tactile* transmission of apostolic succession is not helpful. More importantly, this statement may
not be true. What is required by God for the Eucharist to be
a genuine anamnesis, communion with the Risen Lord, and
gift of his Spirit is mootly discussed by theologians. Each
Church has its own criterion. Would it not be preferable to
find some way of recognizing the Eucharist in each Church

---

[13]George H. Tavard. *A Theology For Ministry*. Wilmington,
Del., Michael Glazier, 1983. p. 101-117.

rather than requiring of them that they fit the procrustean mold of a given Church? Orthodox require of Romans that they drop the "filioque" of the creed before they will recognize their Eucharists. Roman Catholics require that celebrants receive their ordination from bishops who have "tactile" linkage with the apostles. Anglicans and Protestants require rejection of post-reformation dogmas and teachings by the Council of Trent. All of these demands may be both contradictory and unnecessary to God and the Spirit who unites. In God's eyes who is to say that a Eucharist celebrated by a Christian community by its duly ordained celebrant, with the preaching of the word and the invoking of the Spirit is invalid? Can we say it is of no worth, that nothing is accomplished? Would it not be truer to say that because Jesus and his Spirit are in the midst of such an assembly, the Body of Christ is being built, the word is being proclaimed, the Spirit is being given, and communion with the Trinity and among the members of Christ is being achieved? If that be so, then what else is required for the Eucharist to be genuine?[14]

In raising these questions we are not implying that we disagree with Roman Catholic insistence on valid ordination for valid Eucharist. Nor are we hinting that the COCU proposition of laying on of hands for mutual recognition of ministries would not be useful.[15] What we are suggesting is the need for unity and pastoral ministry to the world make it urgent that the mode and means for recognition of Baptism, Eucharist and Ministry be determined at this time so that we can get on with the task of unity. Once the criteria have been established (no small task in the light of so many diverse theologies) and prayerfully agreed upon, there remains the tremendous task of determining what kind of unity is desired, and what kind of unity is possible.

[14]*Ibid.,* esp. p. 109-110 and 115-117.

[15]The COCU Consensus: *In Quest of a Church of Christ Uniting.* Edit. by Gerald F. Moede. Baltimore, COCU, 1985. Ministry #37, p. 47. et al.

The Spirit in the Churches

Rather than dwell on these matters of Church structure, let us turn to the work of the Spirit in the Churches. Vatican II has emphasized that the Spirit dwells in Christians everywhere, and works in the Churches for the salvation of all. Recognizing this work of inspiration and salvation in other Churches can do much to assist both the work of ecumenism and our own spiritual life.

As we have indicated before, Catholics and Protestants have much to learn from the Churches of the East. The Holy Spirit is a more familiar reality in the Liturgy, piety, theology and spirituality of Orthodox and Eastern rite Churches. The patristic heritage is more a part of the Eastern fabric than it is in the West. The Eastern Liturgy is largely that of John Chrysostom or earlier texts which preserve the trinitarian orientation of the Apostolic Church. Christological controversies, especially Arianism, affected the West far more than the East. Many liturgical scholars point out the harmful effect of the Christological focus in reaction to Arianism on Liturgy in the West.[16] Focus on the divinity of Christ rather than his humanity resulted in a lack of trinitarian focus.

The same is true of theology, spirituality and popular devotion. We therefore have much to gain from an exploration of Eastern spirituality, especially as described in the writings of the Fathers of the Church.

The Spirit is at work in the Eastern Churches, and in the measure that Western Christians return to an openness to the Spirit, in that measure are they preparing "from within" the *rapprochement* of Churches East and West.

As for the Churches of the Reformation and the Anglican Communion, these Churches too are open to the Spirit. They can learn from our own openness to the Spirit and charismatic renewal. All must be open and aware of the Spirit working within the Churches and among Christians, moving one and all into the one Body of Christ. As we have

---

[16]e.g. Louis Bouyer. Godfrey Diekmann, O.S.B.

described it above, the work of the Spirit is through the Word and Sacrament, especially the Eucharist, to bring Christians into communion with the Risen Lord and through him with the Trinity. This work continues wherever the Word of God is proclaimed, Christians are baptized and the Risen Lord gathers his Church.

Spiritual ecumenism is a realization of this saving work of the Spirit. Practical ecumenism is the consequent working together with Christian brothers and sisters for the betterment of the human condition in the world in which we live. Peace and justice, human rights, food, shelter and clothing for the needy, education and opportunity for all are so many ways of building God's kingdom and uniting the Body of Christ.

The Eucharist and the Spirit

We might add a word on the Eucharist and the Spirit and Christian unity. We have already described how the Eucharist binds Christians into the Body of Christ by the gift of the Spirit. We would like to draw attention to the fact that this saving action transcends the boundaries of individual Churches.

As Catholics receive the Eucharist they are imperceptibly perhaps, but surely, drawn into communion with brothers and sisters of other Churches. The same is true of Orthodox Christians. Wherever the Lord is present as the Eucharist is celebrated, he gives his Spirit which unites Christians into the Body of Christ.

What of those Churches which celebrate the Lord's Supper without a ministry having apostolic succession? What of those Eucharists considered to be valid within a given Church, but not afforded a recognition as such by other Churches? As we indicated above, there is a need to revise our categories of licit/valid today. Many theologians believe these Eucharists are valid but "illicit" by the standards of other Churches. Thus Jesus is really and truly present wherever legitimately celebrated (i.e., with the intention of doing what the Lord Jesus did and taught his followers to do). If Jesus is present, he surely gives his Spirit to those who are open to receive the Spirit. Thus the Body of Christ is strengthened in love by the gift of divine love.

The medieval theologians developed a concept which might be helpful here. It is the concept of *"spiritual commun-ion."*[17] If one were to hold that only Eucharists celebrated according to, e.g., the Roman Catholic (or Orthodox) standard for validity, one could still admit some fruitfulness to such celebrations. Those who so celebrate at least have the desire to celebrate the Lord's Supper and desire its fruits (charity and the Holy Spirit). Such desire in itself is fruitful. Just as *"spiritual communion"* according to the medieval theologians produced the fruit of sacramental communion, so modern Eucharists which do not meet canonical require-ments for "validity" might very well meet the requirements for a reception of the *"fruits"* of the Sacrament.

We express this opinion *"cogitando, non affirmando"* (thinking, not affirming) as a possible beginning of some appreciation for Eucharists which do not meet our own standards of validity. Yet we prefer George Tavard's and other approaches which would stress that the categories of "valid/licit" are no longer useful in our ecumenical discus-sions. We need to go beyond them. Whatever it would take to recognize each other's Eucharists is what we need to seek. Meanwhile, we ought to recognize that something is happen-ing within the Churches through the Risen Lord and his Spirit—especially through the Eucharist—to make us one in the Body of Christ.

Communion of Hospitality

For this reason we would be encouraged by a develop-ment of hospitality in the matter of the Eucharist. There are

[17]Francis Costa, S.S.S. "Communion, Spiritual" in *New Cath-olic Encyclopedia* vol. 4 p. 39 and "Nature and Effects of Spiritual Communion" *Cath. Theol. Soc.* 13 (1958) 139-148.

pastoral circumstances when spiritual needs dictate the reception of the Eucharist by those outside our own communion. While the new Code of Canon Law allows such reception (under certain conditions) to other than Roman Catholics, reciprocity is allowed only in Churches whose Sacraments "are considered valid" (Canon 844 #2). Without criticizing this determination, we would like to encourage its use. The Eucharist is always a means to unity as well as a sign of the unity which the Spirit produces in the Body of Christ. From a practical point of view the Eucharist as a *means* of unity seems more realistic. Disunity exists everywhere. Within a Church as well as between the Churches. The Eucharist seeks to produce unity among God's children. The Lord and his Spirit continue to unite us in spite of our disunity in the Body of Christ. Hence when communion of hospitality is allowed, its value for ecumenism should not be overlooked.

Pastoral situations which warrant such use of the Eucharist may very well prove a bond of healing for families and the Churches beyond expectations. Pastoral moments are always teachable moments and should be discreetly used to further the Lord's mission of unity.

5

Unity in the Body of Christ
Through the Eucharist

In our discussion of Paul's letter to the Corinthians[1] we stressed that the unity of the Church is the fruit of the Eucharist. The validity of our Eucharist as signs which produce what they signify requires that we work for the unity of the Church if we receive the Eucharist.

We would like to develop that theme more at length in this chapter with a particular stress on recent developments in the ecumenical field, especially with respect to the theology of the Eucharist.

Much Catholic writing stresses the Eucharist as a sign of unity. The impression seems to be that no sharing of the Eucharist is possible until unity between Churches has been achieved. Anglican, Lutheran and Protestant writing (and Church policy) stresses that unity among Christians will always be a fragile reality. The ecumenical movement is a journey toward unity which may be achieved in its final

---

[1]See Chapter Three, *One in Christ's Body* p. 56-66. See also Chapter Four, *The Eucharist and the Holy Spirit.*

stages only in the parousia. Meanwhile we need "Food for the Journey."[2] The Eucharist is the means toward unity to be achieved.

Both of these aspects of the Eucharist are complementary. We need to celebrate in the Eucharist the unity which we achieve. We also need to receive the Eucharist to continue our progress forward.

Across church boundaries Christ unites his Church. The process is a spiritual one, not simply a political or bureaucratic one.[3] The journey to unity is a long one. Many will faint on the way, if they are not nourished by the Bread of Life and the Gift of the Spirit. This Bread and Gift are not limited to one of the Christian Churches. Vatican II indicates that while the Church of Christ subsists in the Catholic Communion, God's word is active in other Churches and Ecclesial Communions. Our ecclesiology has progressed remarkably in the Council. Our sacramentality also needs to grow. Many theologians believe that in the light of present ecclesiology it is possible to agree on the validity of orders and sacraments in other Christian communions.[4] The World Council of Churches in its Faith and Order document *"Baptism, Eucharist and Ministry"* has called for mutual recognition precisely in these terms. The theologians have prepared the way, the Churches need to respond in kind. This process of "reception" will take time. John Paul II[5] has to some extent anticipated this recognition, by saying that even though we celebrate at different altars and in different churches, we are drawn together by the one Christ whom we share "because the bread and the cup are one" (1 Cor 10:17).

[2]See *"Food For The Journey".* EDEO-NADEO, 1985. Albuquerque, N.M.

[3]See Robert Hale. *Canterbury and Rome: Sister Churches* p. 12-47.

[4]See George Tavard. *A Theology For Ministry.* Wilmington, Del. p. 85-86.

[5]John Paul II. *Redemptor Hominis.* Washington, D.C. U.S.C.C. Publ. Office. p. 79-84. See also: Encyclical on the Eucharist.

This unity must grow as we open our hearts and minds to the Spirit who makes the Body one.

While intercommunion between members of the various Churches is a slow and painstaking process, there is room for a transitional reception of the Eucharist often referred to as "communion of hospitality." Under this rubric, persons may receive in Churches other than their own under certain precise conditions.[6] In general the prerequisites stress Baptism, proper intention/preparation, receiving of one's own accord, similar faith in the Eucharist, Sacraments considered to be valid in one's own Church, mutual agreement/dialogue between the Churches concerned, and the avoidance of scandal. In addition one must be unable to receive in one's own Church. Finally, specific pastoral situations must be envisaged and defined by the local bishop.

Weddings and funerals are among the most frequently mentioned pastoral occasions. Special areas or situations, e.g., rural areas without the services of appropriate clergy, military installations, persons confined to institutions are other opportunities.[7]

Rome has already indicated that the Orthodox Church has special consideration where such communion of hospitality is concerned. A recent agreement on intercommunion with the Syrian Orthodox Church is especially significant because of its theological implications.[8] (The Russian Orthodox Church in 1970 agreed to allow Catholics travelling in Russia and other places access to Holy Communion when they would otherwise be deprived.)

The EDEO-NADEO Study on eucharistic sharing, "Food For The Journey" (1985), studies the responses of ecumenical officers in the Catholic and Anglican Churches for their

[6]See Canon 844 and commentaries. James Provost in *Food For The Journey*. Albuquerque, N.M. EDEO-NADEO. 1985 p. 64-78.

[7]See *Food For The Journey* esp. p. 22 and 23.

[8]Catholic-Syrian Orthodox Statement signed by John Paul II and Syrian Orthodox Patriarch Moran Mar Ignatius Zakka I Iwas of Antioch, June 23, 1984.

understanding of present legislation and pastoral needs in their regard.[9] The theological implications of this study are especially important.

Recognition of Anglican Orders and the validity of their Eucharist is important to future ecumenical progress.[10] But even more important is a realization that while our Churches work at mutual recognition, we must mutually recognize each other as members of the Body of Christ. If we recognize that we are members of Christ and that the Spirit lives in us and unites us in one Body, the Eucharist we receive has a real function, namely of making us one. Whenever propriety and pastoral need indicate eucharistic hospitality is possible and permissible, we should see these occasions as oportunities of celebrating the unity that exists across Church lines in the Body of Christ. Though these celebrations of our unity may be infrequent, the reality of that unity should be recognized continually.

Marriage[11]

Marriage, especially in an ecumenical context, deserves special consideration in this regard. Baptized Christians who enter into marriage, symbolize and exemplify the unity/disunity of the Church. Paul sees marriage as the great sign of the relationship between Christ and his Church. The paradigm of human love is precisely the self-sacrificing of Jesus for his Bride, the Church (cf. Eph 5:21-33).

The strained relations between the Christian Churches is dramatized in inter-Church marriages. The Eucharist could be a great balm for healing these tensions, were it permitted

[9]EDEO-NADEO Standing Committee. *"Food For The Journey"*, A Study of Eucharistic Sharing, Albuquerque, N.M. 1985.

[10]See EDEO-NADEO Progress Report 1984 p. 9. See also ARCIC I—Ordained Ministry #17 and Elucidation #6.

[11]See Rene Beaupere. "Double Belonging: Some Reflections". *One In Christ* 18 (1982) p. 31-43.

more widely than at present. It is to be hoped that the pastoral sensitivity to inter-Church marriages will break through the present difficulty.

The Eucharist and Unity Within the Church

While unity between the Churches and its implications for the Eucharist are important, there is also a unity to be created within the Church itself. This unity *"ad intra"* and *"ad extra"* interact on one another. Perceptions in either direction are significant.

Many Christians are alienated from their Churches because of a prevailng idea that the Eucharist is to be received only by those who are "worthy of it." This perception of the Eucharist spread quickly as a result of the anti-Arian response of the Church. The Liturgy stresses the divinity of Christ and the awe and reverence to be paid him especially in the Eucharist. Exaggeration of this reverence reached such a level that the Church required people to receive the Eucharist under pain of sin at least once a year (Council of Lateran IV, 1215 A.D.). Other medieval factors contributed to the idea that only the "pure" need approach the Eucharist.

Clearly one who refuses to ask forgiveness for sin, or who obdurately persists in a sinful practice, needs to make his peace with God before sitting down at his table. However the Roman Catholic obligation to confess one's sins before receiving the Eucharist is of late formulation, and is not without exception even today.[12] It must be understood that this obligation concerns serious or mortal sins, not the offenses of which we are daily guilty.

Jesus had no problem eating with sinners. Precisely by reaching out to them in friendship, he succeeded in changing their lives. Sometimes it seems that the Churches have been more concerned with excommunication than with commun-

[12]cf. Canon #916 of the New Code of Canon Law.

ication. That was not the approach of Jesus. The new Code of Canon Law restricts excommunication to extreme cases. Yet the attitude that the Eucharist is some kind of reward prevails.

St. Peter Julian Eymard suffered a great deal from this attitude which was even more deeply imbedded in the Jansenist atmosphere of his time than today.[13] He could not receive the Holy Eucharist in First Communion until his twelfth year. As a Blessed Sacrament Father, he worked hard at making the practice of the Church more flexible. The Eucharist is a need; not a reward. We receive the Eucharist because we need it, not because we deserve it.

This sane attitude toward the Eucharist could make us much more open to allowing Christians who are today alienated to receive Communion. This is true for those outside our own Church, as well as for those who are within it.

In the Catholic Church, this changed attitude would particularly affect those who are divorced, or who are (in opposition to the Church's official stand on the question) practicing birth control by methods not approved by the Church. On this last point *Humanae Vitae* is much more compassionate and pastorally sensitive than is generally believed. The encyclical sees the possibility of someone making a personal decision contrary to the Church's official teaching in specific circumstances.[14]

Similarly a compassionate attitude toward the marginalized in society is far more consonant with the Spirit of Jesus than the pharisaical attitude sometimes experienced in Christian circles. The healing of sin and restoration of members of the Body of Christ requires an openness to the "less than tidy" members of our broken Body, the Church.

Without advocating indiscriminate use of the Eucharist,

---

[13]See L. St. Pierre. *"L'Heure" du Cenacle dans la vie et les oeuvres de Pierre-Julien Eymard.* Lyon, Lescuyer, 1968. esp. p. 1-42.

[14]Paul VI, Pope. Encyclical *Humanae Vitae.* July 25, 1968. #29. TPS 13 (1968) p. 345. See also #18 and 20 TPS p. 339 and 340.

we are saying it is the poor, the sick, the marginalized, the alienated who especially *need* the Eucharist. And all of us belong to that category of persons more than we are willing to admit. Those who are willing to recognize and admit their own sinfulness, Jesus is able to save. His kingdom continues to expand among these humble folk.

Openness to the Spirit

The ultimate purpose of the Eucharist is to unite us to God in communion and to form one Body. This communion *(koinonia)* is the work of the Holy Spirit. The Risen Lord gives us this Spirit in the Eucharist.

Perhaps the centuries of controversy over the Eucharist might best be understood and resolved with a correct understanding of spiritual communion. The Reformers, stressing the cooperation of the recipient and their preparation for the Eucharist (especially in terms of a hearing and assimilation of God's word in the Scriptures), emphasized the need for personal transformation in Christ. Perhaps we can better understand what John Calvin was driving at in this context.[15] Rather than a denial of the presence of Christ in the Eucharist, he affirmed it would be a mistake to interpret that presence in some *material* sense. Communion, after all, is a spiritual matter between the Christian and the Risen Lord. *"Spiritual Communion"* is therefore more important than the proximity of the host to the recipient. And the ultimate purpose of receiving the Eucharist is so that we might receive the Holy Spirit and thus be united to Christ and the Trinity. The epicletic nature of the Eucharist stresses its transformative value. We do not receive either to be thrilled or rewarded. We receive to be transformed.

The Spirit is at work as the Scriptures are read, as the elements are changed, as the celebrating congregation

[15]John Calvin. *Institutes of the Christian Religion*. tr. by Henry Beveridge. Grand Rapids, Eerdmans, 1957. 2 vols.

becomes one with Christ and with each other. The Spirit is at work as the Risen Lord is received and unites us to the Trinity of Persons in one God.

The Laity and the World

The laity come to the Eucharist to be transformed by the Spirit. But the Spirit also transforms the world. He does so by the saving action of the Risen Lord and by the sanctifying action of grace and the transforming work of the Church in the marketplace.

If the Church is to succeed in its mission to the world, the laity must be empowered to transform the world. The grace of Baptism confers both the mission and the power to be involved in such transformation. The Eucharist nourishes, sustains and refreshes the Body of Christ for its task in the world. That task is essentially service *(diakonia)*. Service means material assistance (feeding the hungry, clothing the naked, giving shelter to the homeless, visiting those in prison—or otherwise confined—comforting the sick, strengthening the dying and burying the dead). It also means spiritual assistance, whether this is of a social or inspirational kind. The laity need to work at the transformation of society by the application of Christian principles to every area of life: business and industry, education and culture, the arts and sciences, etc. Inspired by the Gospel, the laity need to bring God's message of hope and salvation to influence every aspect of living.

The world is to be seen as the place where the kingdom is built. *"Fuga mundi"* (flight from the world) is to be interpreted as an occasional and temporary respite which should lead to greater and renewed involvement in the mission of the Church. We are all part of the continent of human existence. No one can be an isolated island. We are connected and dependent upon one another as members of the Body.

This interdependence makes the Eucharist necessary. The Body of Christ is built up by the one bread and one cup. It cannot grow without such spiritual nourishment: "Unless you eat the flesh of the Son of Man, and drink his blood you cannot have life in you (Jn 6:53).

Learning from Twenty Years of Dialogue

A careful study of bi-lateral theological materials and official statements of theological convergence and consensus makes it clear that a common understanding of the nature of the Eucharist has emerged.[16] At the pastoral and practical level we have come (or are quickly coming) to the conclusion that the Eucharist must become, for all Christians of whatever Church or persuasion, a normal focus of the Christian life. The word of God must lead to the Sacrament of the Eucharist. And the assimilation of the Eucharist must lead to a prayerful study of the Scriptures. Intimate union with Christ through assimilation of his word and Sacrament should lead to a better understanding and zeal for his mission to the world.

Anglican, Lutheran, Roman Catholic understanding of the Eucharist are in agreement about the place of the Eucharist in our lives. Reformed and to some extent Evangelical understanding cover the same ground.

An overstress on the operation of Christ *(opere operato)* on the Catholic side has led to a new emphasis on the work of the recipient *(opere operantis)*. The Protestant stress on the word of God has led to a modern appreciation for the need of Sacraments. These views are not opposed to each other but complementary. Over it all is a new reawakening of the importance of Sacraments for the Christian life.

The World Council of Churches' document on *Baptism, Eucharist and Ministry* stresses both a return to the Scrip-

---

[16]See The COCU Consensus: *In Quest of a Church of Christ Uniting* edit. by Gerald F. Moede, Baltimore, COCU, 1985 for a summary of the present agreement in this area, esp. section on the Lord's Supper p. 37-38.

tures and a wider use of the Eucharist. The document explains both the nature of the Eucharist as the sacramental presence of Christ and the sharing in his sacrifice of redemption. The effects of the Eucharist in terms of social or communitarian concerns in the world are also studied. Thus the Sacraments are seen not as isolated in individualistic rites, but as a communitarian challenge related to the mission of Christ to the world. Worship of God leads to service of men and women.

Bi-lateral dialogues have indicated a development of various aspects of eucharistic spirituality in the several Churches. Each of these complementary developments can be beneficial to all. Insights have been incorporated into both bilateral and multi-lateral statements by the Churches. This common faith is also leading to a common recognition of both Ministry and Eucharist across Church lines.

The laity need to see the Eucharist as a normal focus for Christian living. It is the ebb and flow of action and contemplation. The Eucharist brings the Christian to God in Christ and the Spirit, and to the Christian community in commitment and service. The laity must see the Eucharist as the very presence of the Risen Lord who is God's Word Incarnate. While this reality suggests reverence rather than a casual approach to liturgy and eucharistic prayer, it also suggests a source of grace and life without which the pilgrim Church cannot continue its journey.

The Eucharist is also the source of Christian fellowship *(koinonia)* which is both love and service of others' needs. The Eucharist builds the Christian community while reminding it of "the new commandment" (Jn 13:34) and the example of Jesus' service "unto the end" (Jn 13:1).

In this context the Christian experiences God. The Risen Lord who is present in the assembly and in the proclaimed word, is especially present in the "breaking of bread." "It is I, do not be afraid," the Lord tells us as we receive, confessing that we are indeed unworthy to have him "under our roof." He gives us his Spirit whereby we call God "Abba" (Father). We are united as one Body with our brothers and sisters

living and dead ("we feebly struggling, they in glory. . .").[17]
We receive the Sacrament by which we are saved and
remember the commandment by which we are challenged.
We receive the bread and wine transformed into the Body
and Blood of Christ, and are prepared for the mission of
transforming the world in which we live. . . beginning with
ourselves, and reaching to the ends of the earth.

Through the Eucharist God becomes real for us, as does
the mission of Jesus which we share. Liturgical renewal
needs to parallel Christian involvement at the social level,
and vice versa.[18]

Here again, Protestant and Catholic ethos are complementary. The social Gospel needs a liturgical counterpart.
Liturgy remains sterile if it does not lead to good works and
establishing the reign of God.

---

[17]Hymn *"For All The Saints"* text by William W. How (1823-
1897) verse 3:

O blest communion, fellowship divine!
We feebly struggle, they in glory shine;
Yet all are one in thee for all are thine: Alleluia.

See our article *"The Eucharist and the Communion of the Saints"*—
Priest, vol. 39 p. 29-31 April 1983.

[18]Regis Duffy, O.F.M. develops this theme at length in: *Real
Presence:* Worship, Sacraments, Commitment. N.Y., Harper and
Row, 1982.

6

The Ecumenical Dimension of Eucharistic Spirituality

We have begun to suggest that every Christian Church has much to learn from its sister Churches. Vatican II broke entirely new ground by acknowledging that the Body of Christ was not limited to the Catholic Communion, but also embraced Orthodox, Anglican, Lutheran, Protestant, Evangelical and other Churches and communions as well. God gives his Spirit and his grace in these Christian Churches and ecclesial Communions.[1]

Theologians are fond of pointing out that while unity is the goal of the ecumenical movement, the division of Christians has not been without positive value. Each Church and Communion has developed its own style of Christianity, its own ritual, polity and practice. In the process theological and spiritual insights have been born. Today the many differences among Christians are seen much more in their complementarity and positive value, rather than polemically or antagonistically.

[1] *Unitatis Redintegratio* #3 and 4. Lumen Gentium #8.

Our scope does not permit us to go into detail into the different spiritual insights of the various Churches, and we can only sketch the variety and strengths of these individual insights. However it is important to take at least a passing look at the contributions of the different Communions.

Orthodox Spirituality

The patristic period and later developments are the special focus of the Orthodox Church. Orthodox spirituality is richly liturgical (liturgical texts continuing in the tradition of St. John Chrysostom) and deeply patristic (which is also to affirm its biblical roots). Eastern in flavor, deeply mystical, the Orthodox spirituality has much to teach Western Christians.

Dialogue with Orthodoxy has required a return to patristic and early conciliar sources. Eastern mysticism has its counterpart in the western mystics, and the two are complementary.

Orthodox spirituality has not been tainted with the pessimism characteristic of the Augustinian West. It is filled with a *joie de vivre* reflected in its liturgical settings which fill all the senses: music for the ear, incense for the nostrils, oil-wine-bread for the touch and taste, icons and gestures for the eyes and rich symbolism and prayer for the emotions and one's aesthetic sense. Orthodox spirituality is incarnational and stresses both the resurrection and the world to come. Communion is not only among the faithful who are deeply involved in the Liturgy, but also with the saints and angels with whom the earthly Liturgy joins in songs of praise.

The patristic point of view reflects this liturgy, mysticism and optimism. Close to the golden ages of Greece and Rome, the Fathers of the Church reflect the best of that human tradition transformed by the gospel. While the Middle East has shared deeply in the sufferings of Christ, it also lives with sure hope of final victory in the Resurrection. Thomas Aquinas corrected Augustine and stressed grace building on nature rather than rebuilding it. The Fathers are not involved in this dichotomy. Their perspective is deeply scriptural and human. They are fully aware of philosophy, but seek Christian wisdom. Orthodox spirituality is profoundly mystical. The Holy Spirit (the epicletic dimension) is a very conscious reality in liturgy, prayer and life. Prayer in the East is more contemplative than in the West. Prayer has its own value. It is not necessarily a means to something else. Contemplation of God, praise and thanksgiving are at the heart of prayer. Reparation and petition are also essential, but not necessarily the primary focus. Orthodox spirituality is deeply ascetical, but such asceticism is a preparation and purification of the senses to enable more profound contemplation.

We can learn much from Orthodox theology and spirituality. Pope John Paul II said the Church has been breathing with one lung. It must breathe deeply with both: Eastern and Western spirituality.[2]

Anglican Spirituality

Robert Hale in *"Canterbury and Rome: Sister Churches"*[3] develops at some length the characteristics of Anglican spirituality. He stresses its respect for tradition, its monastic roots and its lay involvement. The latter is especially important to Churches which do not have such a tradition. The Catholic Church has only recently given full stress to lay involvement. Hale underscores that the Church is overwhelmingly lay. If the mission of Christ at the service of the

---

[2]John Paul II, Pope. The Reality, Progress and Problems of Christian Unity (to the Roman Curia, June 28, 1985). #8. *Origins* 15 no. 8, July 18, 1985 p. 128.

[3]Robert Hale. *Canterbury and Rome: Sister Churches:* A Roman Catholic Monk Reflects upon Reunion in Diversity. London, Darton-Longman and Todd, 1982.

world has not been as vigorous as it might, the fault may be in an over-clericalized view of the Church.

Another characteristic of the Anglican Communion is its stress on "comprehensiveness." The Anglican Church tends to open its arms ever more widely so as not to exclude any of its members or their point of view. Though many denominations have arisen from Anglican roots, each of these "branches" took root and survived for some time within Anglicanism. The points of view seem to survive in the Anglican Church even today.

This desire to accommodate varying points of view and insisting only on what is absolutely necessary is characteristic of the early Church. It may well prove a pattern and formula for ecumenical unity in the future.

Lutheran Emphasis[4]

Emphasis on the proclamation of the Word of God is a stress developed especially in the Lutheran and Reformed Churches. Luther's outstanding contribution to Christianity is precisely the need to return to the Scriptures as normative of the Christian life. The presence of the Spirit in the preaching of the Word of God, and its sanctifying power continue to be important dimensions of Lutheran spirituality.

This emphasis on the Scriptures did not eliminate Lutheran stress on Sacraments. Baptism, Eucharist, Reconciliation remain important to Lutheran life. Yet even the celebration of Sacraments are seen as proclamation of God's word and salvation.

[4]See Paul C. Empie. *Lutherans and Catholics in Dialogue:* Personal Notes for a Study. Edit by Raymond Tremeyer. Philadelphia, Fortress Press 1981.   See also the 7 volumes edited by Empie and others reporting dialogue agreement and study papers of the dialogue over the past decade of years.

Reformed (Presbyterian) Spirituality[5]

A Scottish and English development of Calvinism, Presbyterians stress lay ministry and a democratic Church polity. Calvinist insistence on spiritual growth rather than on "materialistic" use of the Sacraments continue to be an important part of Presbyterian spirituality. The doctrine of predestination, softened through experience and a return to the scriptural and patristic sources, is still an important part of the Presbyterian view of things.

In terms of eucharistic spirituality Calvin is an important theologian. At the time of the Reformation his insistence on the *spirit* seemed to deny the real presence of Christ or the tranformation of the elements in the eyes of Roman interpreters. Yet at this distance from the fray, his emphasis is seen rather as an insistence on the task of the recipient and their spiritual growth, rather than a denial of a genuine and true presence of Christ. Such an insistence on the "spiritual" presence of Christ rather than a crass "materialistic" one continues to be an emphasis that is of value.

Methodist Spirituality[6]

An outgrowth of Anglicanism and an effort to return the Anglican Church to its liturgical (eucharistic) roots as well as a deepening of the spiritual life (piety) characterize Methodism even today. American Congregationalism also influenced the United Methodist Church which is the result of several mergers. Methodist polity maintains a lot of Anglican "comprehensiveness" and even goes beyond it.

[5]See *The Encyclopedic Dictionary of Western Churches.* Edit by T.C. O'Brien. Washington/Cleveland, Corpus Publishers, 1970 articles "Reformed Churches" p. 654-656; and "Presbyterianism" p. 617-619. Also "Calvinism" p. 121-126.

[6]See *The Encyclopedic Dictionary of Western Churches.* Articles "Methodism" p. 489-491; and "Wesley, John" p. 799-801.

Perhaps one of the outstanding contributions of the Methodist Church is its hymnology. The Wesley brothers found that large numbers of simple people could be quickly taught the essentials of the faith and spirituality through hymns. Many of these hymns are used in all Churches and denominations. The Roman Catholic Church in the USA found these hymns especially valuable as it looked for vernacular material for the Vatican II Liturgy.

Congregational Spirituality[7]

The Congregational Church (which has undergone a number of mergers in recent years) is identified with New England towns and the Pilgrims who settled the area. The Church stressed the autonomy of the local congregations and its importance to the development of the spirituality. Coming from Anglican roots the Church conserved a democratic polity. It also has roots in the Reform movement and its insistence on the Scriptures. Comprehensiveness is also visible in Congregational spirituality today. (In my own experience I found Congregational members generally siding on respect for the individual and a creative or democratic view rather than a traditional or "trendy" position.)

Baptist Emphasis[8]

The Baptist view is probably best exemplified by the conservative Southern Baptist Church. Followers of Zwingli (he represents the other side of the coin in the Reformation), Baptists emphasize the literal interpretation of the Bible as normative. The autonomy of the local congregation prevails.

[7]See *The Encyclopedic Dictionary of Western Churches.* Articles "Congregationalism" p. 225-227.

[8]See *The Encyclopedic Dictionary of Western Churches.* Article "Baptists" p. 72-74.

Adult Baptism by immersion, after profession of faith is also characteristic.

The Baptist contribution to Christianity is its insistence on baptismal spirituality. Baptism requires faith, rebirth in Christ, and a lifetime commitment to the way of the Gospel. (In my experience Baptists resemble Roman Catholics of the pre-Vatican II days. They insist theirs is the only true Church. They rebaptize a great deal.)

Zwingli carried to its extreme the idea that the Eucharist is fruitful depending on the response of the individual. He denied anything but a spiritual effect of the Sacrament. And he reduced the Sacraments of the Church to Baptism and Eucharist.

The Baptist Communion retains many of the emphases of other Protestant groups. They are the least attached to oral tradition and squarely opt for the written word.

Overview

If one tries to see these emphases as interconnected rather than adversary, one can see there is much to learn from each contribution. Chesterton in *Orthodoxy* explained that remaining true to the Gospel is a tight-rope walking.[9] Newman made the same comparison in speaking of theology. It is difficult to keep one's balance. But balance is the sign of orthodoxy. Keeping the truth and developing our understanding of it requires a tightrope balancing act. Each Church and denomination is in danger of exaggerating one point of view. Other Churches can help to maintain a balance. History will show that what was first seen as heresy, after purification in the crucible of reaction, eventually was absorbed in the corrected view of orthodoxy.

[9]Gilbert Keith Chesterton. *Orthodoxy*. London, Bradley Head, 1949. 278p. The Paradoxes of Christianity, p. 131-169. Esp. p. 166-169.

Applying these insights to the present renewal of the Church and spirituality we find a series of emphases which can help the Church today.

Liturgical and Lay Movements

Though each of the Churches has had its own development of spirituality, liturgy and lay involvement, some of these movements have crossed Church lines in recent decades. The biblical, patristic, theological, lay, social and peace movements are common to the entire Christian world. The ecumenical movement has resulted in a greater sharing of all of these movements in Chrstianity. Seminarians and deacon training courses are done in theological school clusters. Continuing education of clergy and laity similarly are done in an ecumenical setting in many instances.

The liturgical movement and the movement toward greater lay involvement are of particular importance. Failure to fully appreciate the liturgical life of the Church or the importance of fully involving the laity are not defects of one Church alone. To a lesser or greater degree they afflict all of Christianity. The ecumenical movement is valuable because it improves the entire Body of Christ.

The World Council of Churches' Faith and Order document on *Baptism, Eucharist and Ministry* (BEM) is a call to each Christian Church to deepen its spirituality and theology of Baptism, Eucharist and all Ministries, lay and ordained. Mutual recognition is also key to the future unity of the Church. In the meantime we can grow together.

Openness to the Spirit

We have stressed the epicletic dimension of the Orthodox Church. Openness to the Spirit is a growing phenomenon in the West as well. The Charismatic Movement is but one aspect of this openness. All of us are becoming more aware of our need to discern the movements of the Spirit and the signs of the times. God speaks to us through both. The Spirit is important to the liturgy celebrated and the word proclaimed and understood. The discernment of the Spirit is a classical task for Christians whatever their affiliation or persuasion. This openness seems especially imperative in this age of ecumenism and rediscovery of the importance of the Eucharist to modern spiritual growth.

The Eucharist and Ecumenical Spirituality

With regard to the Eucharist, the *BEM* calls for renewal in all the Churches, and proposes several areas for growth. Of particular interest to us is the social dimension of the Eucharist. If we celebrate the Lord's Supper we are challenged to bring God's word and grace to the world in which we live. We need to build the Body of Christ if we are its members; we need to build God's kingdom if we are nourished for the life to come.

Eucharistic spirituality means contemplation of God's word and God's will. We receive the Bread of Life to be nourished with God's grace and Spirit.

There is a growing awareness of the place of the Eucharist in the life of the Church. This book is intended to focus on some aspects of this truth. Our hope is that our readers will see the need to work at the unity of the Churches as we receive the Bread that makes us one with Christ and with each other. Genuine eucharistic renewal must be ecumenical renewal at the same time, and to the same degree.

Renewal: a Change of Attitude

We need to emphasize again that spiritual renewal involves a change of attitudes. The Churches cannot become one without a profound change of attitude on the part of all its members. The Body cannot be one unless all its members are one. One heart and mind characterized the early Christian community. "See how these Christians love one another." In spite of their differences—which were many—the unity of the Christians was so outstanding as to draw all those with whom they came into contact. The mission of Jesus to unite the world can succeed only in the measure that Christians grow in unity.

The Eucharist is at the heart of this growth in unity. The Eucharist cannot be a private thing. We cannot be united to Christ only vertically. We must be united with him horizontally as well, i.e. with Christ in our neighbor, in his members.

The Eucharist is profoundly engaged in the Church's task of renewal and unity. It is inconceivable that this movement toward unity can succeed without the Eucharist.

This is why we are firmly convinced that the *use* of the Eucharist as a means of unity is imperative. Unity will always be fragile and partial. We cannot wait until full communion is achieved in all other matters before the Eucharist is shared. Our Protestant brothers and sisters realized that fact some time ago. The Anglican Church which maintained the same discipline as the Catholic Church not too long ago realized the pastoral and ecumenical need to extend Eucharistic hospitality. In a courageous move both the Anglican and Lutheran Communions achieved a similar policy of eucharistic hospitality.[10] The Syrian Orthodox and Catholic Church reached an agreement on eucharistic hospitality without full communion. *BEM* expresses the hope that similar agreements may be achieved throughout Christendom. This achievement would do much to further the cause of Christian unity.

But beyond these written accords is the need for genuine renewal and transformation of attitudes in the people and in the Churches. Old stereotypes and prejudices must cease to be propagated and reflected in our literature and spoken words. Genuine trust must be cultivated and good intentions

[10]For the Anglican Statement see *Food For The Journey*, Appendix p. 83 and 87.

must be presumed. Fear must give way to trust; alienation to love, disunity to unity in Christ.

Fear and Peace in Spirituality

"Love casts out fear" we are told in the Gospel. Peace is the result of harmonious relations within every individual and in their relationships with God and neighbor. There can be no spiritual life worthy of the name without peace and love in the individual. Peace and love are extremely important to the spiritual life.

Religious prejudice thrives on ignorance, fear, and hatred. We cannot love what we do not know. And so education is very important to the ecumenical movement. We cannot begin to love Christians in other Churches until we get to know more about them. This knowledge is both intellectual and practical. We must learn about our separated brothers and sisters. We must also get to know them personally. Every opportunity must be used, and some must be created.

Such knowledge will eliminate the fear we have of the unknown. Love of our brothers and sisters will cast out fear which makes prejudice thrive.

Finally peace will begin to reign as our relationships improve and are deepened by love and mutual appreciation. I know of no more powerful help than the Eucharist for bringing peace and love to the human heart. The Sacrament of Love and the Sacrament of Peace are the gift of the Risen Lord who gives us the Spirit of Love and who reconciles us to our Father in heaven and our brother/sister on earth.

7

Eucharistic Sacrifice and Gift of Self

The Eucharist as Sacrifice has been a bone of controversy since the Reformation. Protestants emphasize the once-for-all *(ephapax)* character of the Sacrifice of Christ on Calvary, finding their justification in the Epistle to the Hebrews. Catholics stress the *reality* of the Eucharist as Sacrifice, and its *sacramentality.* "Sacraments produce what they signify"—*causant significando,* i.e. have an effective causality as signs.[1] The Protestant view is strongly biblical, the Catholic view is strongly theological and liturgical.

The Reformers were largely reacting to a nominalist theology which stresses "what you see is what you get."[2] Counter-Reformation theology understood the excesses of nominalism and turned to Thomas Aquinas for a solution. His strong metaphysics was just what was needed to underscore the reality and sacramentality of the Eucharist. Some-

---

[1] Thomas Aquinas. *Summa Theologica.* IIIa q. 62 a. 1 ad 1m.

[2] See ARC/USA papers delivered in New York Oct. 13-16, 1985 by Charles Price and Fred Jelly, O.P.

how a lesser brand of scholasticism followed Trent and continued the controversy of the Eucharist, one or many. Catholic theology improved its work in recent decades by both a return to the Scriptures and an emphasis on the one eternal Sacrifice of Christ. The eternal dimension of that Sacrifice is seen as underlying every eucharistic celebration.[3] The *how* of the eucharistic Sacrifice remains a mystery to all. However recent ecumenical dialogues and post-Vatican II theology have brought about a healthy consensus.[4]

Biblical Insights

R. De Vaux in his marvelous study of Old Testament sacrifice[5] points out that their underlying value was not in appeasing an "angry God." Though at times those who offer sacrifice may seem to have that intention, still a deeper study of the essence of sacrifice reveals that the heart of the matter is the self-offering to God of the person sacrificing.

This perception is surely emphasized by later prophetic comments which describe God as displeased with mere lip service or reliance on the offering of animals.

> Ps. 51: Offerings and holocausts of bull offerings you did not want. A humble, contrite heart you will not spurn.[6]

Not the material sacrifice, but the intention of the offerer is important.

The core of religion is what lies in the heart of the individual. It is not in the externals of sacrifice or prayer.

---

[3]Odo Casel. *The Mystery of Christian Worship.* ed. B. Neunheuser, Tr. I.T. Hale, Westminster, Md. Newman, 1962.

[4]See esp. ARCIC. *The Final Report.* Eucharist #5; W.C.C. Faith and Order Commission *Baptism, Eucharist, Ministry.* Eucharist #5-13; and (U.S.) *Lutherans and Catholics in Dialogue* vol. 3 and 4.

[5]R. De Vaux. *Les Sacrifices de l'Ancien Testament.* Paris, 1964.

[6]Hosea 6:6.

New Testament Insights

Jesus teaches ever more clearly what the Old Testament only begins to say. Sacrifice without love is useless. Genuine sacrifice is essentially self-oblation to the will of God. Jesus exemplifies this self-offering in his own life, especially in his ultimate sacrifice for the love of all on Calvary.

If you bring your gift to the altar and there recall that your brother has anything against you, leave your gift at the altar, go first to be reconciled with your brother, and then come and offer your gift (Matt 5:23-24).

Wherefore, on coming into the world, Jesus said:

"Sacrifice and offering you did not desire, but a body you have prepared for me; holocausts and sin offering you took no delight in. Then I said, 'As is written of me in the book, I have come to do your will, O God.'"

First he says:

"Sacrifices and offerings, holocausts and sin offerings, you neither desired not delighted in." (These are offered according to the prescriptions of the law.)

Then he says:

"I have come to do your will."

In other words, he takes away the first covenant to establish the second.

By this 'will' we have been sanctified through the offering of the body of Jesus Christ once for all. Every other priest stands ministering day by day, and offering again and again those same sacrifices which can never take away sins. But Jesus offered one sacrifice for sins and took his seat forever at the right hand of God; now he waits until his enemies are placed beneath his feet. By one offering he has forever perfected those who are being sanctified"(Hebrews 10:5-15).

Paul in his epistles, reflects his understanding of the Master's teaching. Especially in Philippians he exhorts us to have "the mind of Christ":

> "Have this mind in you which was in Christ Jesus. Though he was in the form of God, he did not deem equality with God something to be grasped at. Rather, he emptied himself and took the form of a slave, being born in the likeness of men. He was known to be of human estate, and it was thus that he humbled himself, obediently accepting even death, death on a cross! Because of this, God highly exalted him and bestowed on him the name above every other name. So that at Jesus' name every knee must bend in the heavens, on the earth, and under the earth, and every tongue proclaim to the glory of God the Father: JESUS CHRIST IS LORD" (Phil 2:5-11).

Ecumenical Controversy

The controversy of the Reformation centers largely in the Epistle to the Hebrews. Today Catholics and Protestants alike believe that Hebrews has the last word. Christ's Sacrifice is sufficient for the salvation of all. There can be no "new" sacrifice to complete that one. The Eucharist is, the Council of Trent[7] underscored it, the *same* Sacrifice. The manner of offering alone is different.

But the manner of offering is very important. For some time Catholic theologians were fond of trying to point out some kind of "unbloody" offering in the Eucharist.[8] They saw in the separate words of consecration, a kind of "immolation" and their theology told them that what was signified was done. As far as it goes this theology has some value. The problem is that it does not go far enough. Moreover it is far

[7]Council of Trent. Session XXII. Dz 938 ff.

[8]E.J. Kilmartin. *Eucharist (Sacrifice)* NCE. vol. 5, p. 609-615.

too nominalistic to suit present times, nor does it sufficiently answer the need to show how the Eucharist is the same Sacrifice as that of Calvary.

Dom Odo Casel[9] brought Catholic theology in line with its scriptural roots. He thought some elements of mystery cults might be useful, given a Christian interpretation. Discarding undesirable elements of mystery cults, he found value in some of their insights.

Casel stressed the eternal dimension of the Sacrifice of Jesus. Because he is the Son of God, his actions are theandric. That is, they have both a divine and human dimension. As a human being Jesus could only die once, at a specific time in history, and under restricted circumstances of time, place, persons, etc.

However in its divine dimension the Sacrifice of Jesus is available for the salvation of all. For redemption to happen, it must somehow be available or appropriated by each generation. Every person must "enter into" the Sacrifice of Jesus, or make it his or her own. This can be done because Jesus

> "...on the night before he suffered, took bread, broke it and gave it to his disciples and said: 'Take and eat this all of you. This is my body broken for you...' Take and drink. This is the cup of my blood shed for you and for the remission of sins. Do this in my memory" (1 Cor 11:23-26).

The Eucharist as the memorial *(anamnesis)* of Jesus and the Sacrifice of the Church makes it possible for Christians to share in the once-for-all Sacrifice of Calvary.

While the Eucharist as Sacrifice still remains a matter of controversy, there is a growing consensus in the making. *BEM* states:

> "The eucharist is the memorial of the crucified and risen Christ, i.e., the living and effective sign of his sacrifice, accomplished once and for all on the cross and still

[9]Odo Casel. op. cit.

operative on behalf of all humankind...The *anamnesis* in which Christ acts through the joyful celebration of his Church is thus both representation and anticipation. It is not only a calling to mind of what is past and of its significance. It is the Church's effective proclamation of God's mighty acts and promises...
In Christ we offer ourselves as a living and holy sacrifice in our daily lives (Rom 12:1; 1 Pet 2:5); this spiritual worship, acceptable to God, is nourished in the eucharist, in this we are sanctified and reconciled in love, in order to be servants of reconciliation in the world" (BEM/ Euch.#5-10).

ARCIC's *The Final Report* goes further:

"Christ's redeeming death and resurrection took place once and for all in history. Christ's death on the cross, the culmination of his whole life of obedience, was the one, perfect and sufficient sacrifice for the sins of the world. There can be no repetition of or addition to what was then accomplished once for all by Christ. Any attempt to express a nexus between the sacrifice of Christ and the eucharist must not obscure this fundamental fact of the Christian faith. Yet God has given the eucharist to his Church as a means through which the atoning work of Christ on the cross is proclaimed and made effective in the life of the Church. The notion of *memorial* as understood in the passover celebration at the time of Christ,—i.e., the making effective in the present of an event in the past— has opened the way to a clearer understanding of the relationship between Christ's sacrifice and the eucharist. The eucharistic memorial is no mere calling to mind of a past event or of its significance, but the Church's effectual proclamation of God's mighty acts. Christ instituted the eucharist as a memorial *(anamnesis)* of the totality of God's reconciling action in him. In the eucharistic prayer the Church continues to make a perpetual memorial of Christ's death, and his members, united with God and one another, give thanks for all his mercies, entreat the ben-

efits of his passion on behalf of the whole Church, participate in these benefits and enter into the movement of his
self-offering" (ARCIC #5).

A similar statement can be found in the Lutheran-
Catholic agreed statement (USA) in its declaration on the
Eucharist as Sacrifice.[10]

These agreed statements resolve, at least in part, the tensions in theology of several centuries. They indicate on both
sides an effort and a success in resolving the two sides of the
issue: how the Eucharist is something more than symbolic,
genuinely related to the Sacrifice of Christ, and this without
being somehow a repetition of the immolation of Calvary.

Theological Synthesis

The theological synthesis in the area of the Eucharist as
Sacrifice rests on the notion of memorial or *anamnesis.*[11]
The Eucharist is a Sacrifice in the sense that it is a real
though liturgical re-presentation of the Sacrifice of Christ.
This re-presentation is not a reenactment of the "blood and
gore" of Calvary (as was sometimes thought), but of the
deeper essential ingredient of that historic moment, namely,
the self-offering of Jesus to the Father. It was precisely this
self-offering that was pleasing, not the bloody slaughter. The
Father who loves his Son could not have acted otherwise.
Jesus had said:

> "Greater love than this no one has, than to lay down his
> life for his friends" (Jn 15:13).

---

[10]*Lutherans and Catholics in Dialogue.* vol. III. *The Eucharist
As Sacrifice* esp. p. 188-191.

[11]See ARCIC. *The Final Report* and WCC. *BEM.* and related
materials.

Paul says further:

"It is not easy to die even for a good man—though of course for someone really worthy, a man might be prepared to die—but what proves that God loves us is that Christ died for us while we were still sinners" (Rom 5:6-10).

Further this theological synthesis stresses that the core of the liturgical offering is both the self-offering of Christ, the Head, and the self-offering of his members, the Church. Without this Christian self-offering, the sacrifice is mere lip-service and ritual.

Zwingli's insistence on the symbolic nature of the Eucharist, we believe, is an over-reaction to the nominalistic and ritualistic realism of the Catholic side at the time of the Reformation. His contribution is not without worth, especially as we seek to reestablish the balance of orthodoxy.[12]

Gift of Self

Since the personal gift-of-self of each Christian is so important to the Eucharist as Sacrifice, let us now examine the nature of this gift as it is described in the history of spirituality, especially the French School of Spirituality. We believe this school is especially important because it developed a unique way of understanding the gift of self and also because this school was the antecedent of St. Peter Julian Eymard who has particular "expertise" in the area of the Eucharist and the gift of self.

We recognize that both the manner of speaking of the French School (and even of St. Eymard) is foreign to our way of speaking today. Yet, as in many other matters of spirituality, the theological substance needs always to be

[12]"Zwingli, Huldrych" in *The Encyclopedic Dictionary of the Western Churches*. Edit. by T.C. O'Brien. Washington, Corpus Publ., 1970. p. 819-820.

gleaned and freed from its cultural and linguistic embodiment. Without such a process spiritual writers and schools of spirituality would have a very fleeting value. The underlying theology of any school (and also of individual spiritual writers) is what has permanent value.

With these reflections in mind we can study the French School, especially Olier, and then consider Eymard. St. Eymard was raised in the French School, and quotes Olier verbatim in his great Retreat of Rome (1864);[13] he moved toward the Salesian spirituality in his later years due to the Marist influence and his eucharistic orientation.

Cardinal de Berulle started the French School of Spirituality. His main thrust was the virtue of religion and the mystery of the Incarnation of Christ. For him the important fact of the Incarnation was that with the coming of Christ it is now possible to give to God genuine and full worship, the kind that is both worthy of God and entirely pleasing to him. Before the Incarnation such worship was not possible. God accepted the worship of the Jewish Community as the best that could be offered. It was true because offered not to idols or creatures, but to the one and only God. Yet it was incomplete because God himself intended a more perfect worship in Christ.

Guardini's reflections on the Eucharist echo these sentiments of the French School.[14] These ideas are also reflected in Pius XII's "Mediator Dei" which formed the background for Vatican II's statement on Liturgy.

The virtue of religion was cardinal for de Berulle and other members of the French School. It regulates the worship due to God. (St. Eymard in several drafts of the Constitutions of the Congregation of the Blessed Sacrament indicated that religion was the "characteristic" virtue of the

---

[13]Herve Thibault, S.S.S. *Saint Eymard's Long Retreat of Rome.* 25 January—30 March, 1865. New York, Sentinel Press, 1985. esp. p. 38-43.

[14]Romano Guardini. *Meditations Before Mass,* Westminster, Md. trans. by Elinor C. Briefs. Newman, 1956.

Congregation. As we indicated in our doctoral dissertation,[15] this was a practice very much in vogue at his time. Somehow each community had to have something different in its spirituality. A characteristic virtue was necessary. Later Eymard understood that religion was not sufficiently central to his spirituality and therefore opted for the virtue of charity.)

Olier picked up the thread from de Berulle and made the Eucharist the center of his spiritual edifice. If true religion was offered by the Son of God and he is *the* priest by virtue of his Incarnation, then the Eucharist which re-presents Jesus' supreme act of worship on Calvary (the final extension of his gift of self in the Incarnation), then imitating the self-gift of Christ in the Eucharist should be, for the Christian, the central act of Christian spirituality. Olier favored a single gift of self that would be a total commitment for life. On the other hand he saw the importance of repeating this gift, or rather renewing it in the Eucharistic Sacrifice.

This gift of self became a centerpoint for the spirituality of St. Peter Julian Eymard. His canonization by Pope John XXIII after the first session of Vatican II (and the promulgation of the Decree on Liturgy, *Sacrosanctum Concilium*) indicates the enduring value of his insights. An examination of his inspiration shows that he is at the very heart of eucharistic spirituality and theology.

The Eucharist is the self-offering of Jesus to the Father, *memorialized* in ritual, made available to Christians. The self-offering of Christ calls for the self-offering of Christians. The members of the Body of Christ offer themselves as Christ, the head of the Body, offers himself.

[15]Ernest Falardeau, S.S.S. *Eucharistic Service in the Writings of Peter Julian Eymard*. Rome, Pontifical Gregorian University, 1959. (Part I is published—Part 2 is yet unpublished). We discuss this point in Part I p. 46-49.

Post-Vatican Spirituality

Regis Duffy in *Real Presence* develops the idea of commitment involved in the Sacraments. He especially sees commitment as a necessary part of Baptism. He extends that idea to other Sacraments, in particular to the Eucharist.[16] Robert Kress in *The Church: Communion, Sacrament, Communication*[17] draws the social implications and dimensions of this same reality. We draw attention to the French School not because we need to go back to its formulation, but because its insights remain valid and are reformulated in post-Vatican terms by contemporary theologians.

Bernard Lonergan indicates that this "transculturation" is the basic task of theologians.[18] David Tracy develops this line of thinking in a breath-taking revisionist theology appropriate to the intellectual development of our time.[19] In this sense we would like to draw out the implications of the new (and yet old) theology of the Eucharist for contemporary spirituality. Spirituality today needs to be anchored in a solid theology. It needs also to "read the signs of the times" and to inspire people who are busy in transforming today's world in the light of their faith in Christ.

Against a temptation to return to a pessimistic Augustinianism of a century ago, the full flower of Vatican II needs to move forward with its Incarnational/Resurrectional thrust toward preparing the world for the second coming of Christ by a transformation of the world. Before the Lord can come again, the blind must see, the deaf hear, and the poor must

[16]Regis Duffy, O.F.M. *Real Presence: Worship, Sacraments and Commitment.* San Francisco, Harper and Row, 1982. esp. p. 133-155.

[17]Robert Kress. *The Church: Communion, Sacrament, Communication.* New York, Paulist Press, c.1985. p. 217.

[18]Bernard J.F. Lonergan, S.J. *Method in Theology.* New York, Seabury, 1972.

[19]David Tracy. *Blessed Rage for Order: The New Pluralism in Theology.* New York, Seabury, 1975. 271 p.

know the Gospel. Commitment and dedication to building the reign of Christ are needed. The gift of self is the heart of such commitment in faith.

St. Peter Julian Eymard centered his spirituality on the virtue of religion lived out in love of God and neighbor. He worked for the poor rag-pickers of Paris and prepared them to receive the Lord in the Eucharist.[20] His own celebration of the Eucharist was an opportunity to renew the gift of himself so as to put on Christ and serve him in those in need.

During his long Retreat in Rome (1864)[21] he made a serious personal vow which he called the gift of personality. He wanted to identify with the gift of Jesus to the Word of God. To Eymard's understanding at the moment of the Incarnation Jesus surrendered his humanity to the Divine Word. This gift of self or personality was the pattern for every Christian. (In this sense, Eymard was following the French School.) There must be a total surrender of self to God, so that God's will may be fulfilled in the Christian.

Following Olier, Eymard wanted each Eucharist to be a renewal of this gift.

While, as we have been saying, we might want to phrase our spirituality differently today, the essence of what we need to do in life, and in the Eucharist, is to give ourselves with Christ to God.

Life and Worship — Faith and Action

The Eucharist is a proclamation of God's Word and the good news of salvation for the human race in Christ. The Eucharist proclaims that we are no longer held in the bondage of sin, but are liberated for the service of God and our fellow human beings. Such freedom of the children of God opens our lives to intimate communion with Christ and

[20]F. Trochu. *Le Bx. P.J. Eymard.* Paris, 1949. p. 212-229. *L. St. Pierre. L'Heure du* Cénacle. Lyon, Lescuyer, 1968. p. 241-254.

[21]Herve Thibault, S.S.S. op. cit.

through him with the Trinity and with all the members of the Body of Christ.

Each of these aspects of the Eucharist deserves much consideration.[22] We can only say a brief word here. As proclamation, the Eucharist is the celebration of what we proclaim by our lives daily. We have heard and believed the good news that God comes to his people with salvation. Jesus proclaimed the reign of God "in our midst" (Mt 12:28) and it was the theme of his teaching ministry. We cannot celebrate the central mystery of our faith and redemption, without continuing this proclamation. It is insufficient for us to make a verbal proclamation. Actions speak louder than words, and so our prophetic living is ultimately the response of the challenge of the Eucharist to proclaim the paschal mystery of the Lord.

As liberation, the Eucharist is celebrated "for the forgiveness of sins." As the Eucharist is offered, we are put in touch with the eternal dimension of the salvific action of Jesus Christ. The eternal sacrifice touches the Church and our lives. The liberation given us is real and efficacious. It is both God's gift and our response in openness to our encounter with Christ who encouraged us to *"do this"* in his memory "for the forgiveness of sins" (Mt 26:28).

Our liberation from sin opens us to the possibility of intimate communion with God. We have described that communion in other parts of this book. Suffice it to recall here that such communion is related to our proclamation of the Gospel by our lives, our liberation from sin, and our service to the world.

As liberation theology demonstrates so convincingly, the liberation of Jesus goes beyond personal sin. Through the healing of personal sin, Jesus also helps us to heal and liberate our world from sinful structures that paralyze society and prevent the reign of God's grace from being established in our world, to the glory of God.

[22]Eugene LaVerdiere, S.S.S. has developed this "slogan" of the Congregation of the Blessed Sacrament in a large number of articles in *Emmanuel* over the past several years.

For communion to be possible we must be open to God. The gift of self is the basis for such openness to God. It is part of the process of abnegation which roots the Christian life in charity. Without this negative purification God cannot fully reign in our hearts in love. Jesus himself is described as undergoing a *kenosis* (Phil 2:5-11), and we too must undergo a similar process of detachment/abnegation.

The gift of self is, therefore, a loving and total gift of one's entire self, so that the Father may send his Spirit to transform us, in the likeness of his Son, Jesus Christ, and fill us with the Son's life and redeeming grace.

Religion in Worship

One of the frequent complaints about the post-Vatican II liturgical reform is its casualness. Reverence and respect seem to be absent from many liturgical celebrations. The emphasis on participation and "being oneself" has sometimes given rise to a casualness in celebration and a folksy kind of artistic embellishment that leaves much to be desired.

The corrective is, at least in part, a recognition that love and religion (as described by Thomas Aquinas in the Summa)[23] need to flower into the kind of reverence that breathes faith and genuine worship of God.

Liturgy without these ingredients is lip-service, sham or magic. As we have been saying about the eucharistic celebration, the heart of the matter is the presence of love, reverence, "religion," self-offering, abnegation, and union with God in Christ.

Liturgy has been described as the ebb and tide of life.[24] The accent should be on life. If our lives are Christian the possibility of genuine worship is real. Without a Christian

[23]Thomas Aquinas. *Summa Theologica* II-II q. 82.

[24]Edward Schillebeeckx. *Christ the Sacrament of Encounter With God.* Kansas City, Sheed, 1963 p. 200-215.

life, worship is lacking its deepest meaning. Life and worship are two sides of a single coin.

We need to explore this inner disposition to worship because it is so vital to the Christian life. What we offer to God must be our lives. First Peter long ago underscored this aspect of Christian worship.[25] While worship has its own value and dynamic, this value and dynamic is intimately linked to one's inner dispositions and attitude in life. Faith, hope/trust and love are the very core of both life and worship. What the Lord sees most of all is the heart of our worship.

Contemplation in Action

The ready temptation to divorce life and worship can also be a temptation to separate action and contemplation. The first such dichotomy has to do with the celebration of Eucharist itself, as we have been explaining.

The second dichotomy is between prayer and life. A spirit of prayer must underlie our liturgy. Liturgy must be prolonged, developed, and nurtured by prayer behind closed doors and in the intimacy of one's private life. (This is not to say that the quiet chapel or church is not supremely appropriate for prayer. Indeed it is the normal setting for the kind of prolonged eucharistic reflection we are discussing).[26]

Prayer must be as normal to the Christian as breathing. For those who center their lives on the Eucharist, there is an added reason for prayer. This reason is that the Eucharist itself creates and calls for an atmosphere of prayer. Without such an atmosphere of prayer, much is lost.

Moreover the Christian life itself calls for contemplation. Contemplation is both independent of action and involved with it. Contemplation, in other words, has its own value

[25]I Peter 2:4-10.

[26]S.C.R. *Eucharisticum Mysterium,* 25 May, 1965 esp. ch. 3 #49-51, 53 and 58.

and dynamics. Yet contemplation is intimately related to action and they are mutually related. Action requires contemplation, and contemplation requires action *(contemplata aliis tradere)*.

Thomas Merton[27] and many others in our time, recall the need for contemplation in a hyper-active society and Church. Without such contemplation, the Christian life has no depth. It is like a tree without roots, a house without a solid foundation. For action to be truly, fully, and continuously Christian, it must be sustained by prayerful contemplation of God's word, and the proclamation that is the Eucharist.

If we are to discern the signs of the times, and God's will for us, we must contemplate, i.e., see beyond the surface humdrum of life God's will at work, the Spirit calling and challenging us to action. We must be able to discern the kind of action and the appropriate attitudes required by God and the Spirit.

The Eucharist is not merely celebrated, it is also the focus of Christian prayer. Roman Catholic spirituality has developed a variety of devotions centered on the Eucharist. There are those who believe such a development is unfortunate. We believe that after the corrective measures of pre-Vatican and post-Vatican theology, such devotions have their legitimate place in the Christian life. Many of our Christian brothers and sisters agree.

Both the ARCIC discussions and those surrounding the *BEM* have focused to some extent on this subject.[28] We do not want to develop them at length. But we do believe that one's evaluation of eucharistic devotions should be based on their theological underpinnings, and the long tradition in the Church argues for their existence. Though they were disputed in the Reformation, it was especially the abuses some-

[27]Thomas Merton. *No Man Is an Island.* New York, Harcourt, 1955.

[28]ARCIC, *The Final Report.* Eucharistic Doctrine, #8, 9. WCC. *Baptism, Eucharist, Ministry.* Eucharist #32.

times surrounding these devotions that were particularly at issue.

St. Peter Julian Eymard and many others have developed a rich tradition of eucharistic prayer which would need to be explored by the reader. In briefest terms such devotion consists of contemplating God's word and action, especially the proclamation-liberation-communion which are the Eucharist, in the presence of, or surrounding the bread/wine consecrated and received. The purpose of such contemplation is to draw the greatest fruit from the celebration and sacramental reception of the Eucharist.[29]

We might enlarge on this perception by also considering the effects of the Eucharist in uniting the Body of Christ. While the Churches are divided and we celebrate and receive the Eucharist in various ways, underlying all of them is a deep desire to be united to Christ, to the Trinity and to each other in love and Christian *koinonia*. This effect of the Eucharist is achieved across Church lines and in spite of debate about the validity of orders, or the sacramentality of what we do.[30]

Eucharistic contemplation is therefore an intimate and necessary part of celebrating and receiving the Eucharist. It is a necessary part of life and effective Christian action. Such contemplation will lead inevitably to faith and action.

Faith in Action

The classic debate between faith and good works comes to mind as we seek to round out our vision of the Eucharist. The Eucharist is the *"mysterium fidei"* (mystery of faith). Our faith is challenged to recognize the Lord in the breaking of bread (Lk 24:35). We must also recognize the Lord in those who have no bread.

[29]S.C.R. *Eucharisticum Mysterium* #49-51, 58, 60.

[30]John Paul II, Pope. *Redemptor Hominis* (First Encyclical), March 4, 1979 #20.

The problem of the Reformers about good works was not about their necessity, but their relationship to salvation. The crude view of many at the time was that salvation might be purchased in the way indulgences were bought or sold. The Reformation answer was an insistence that salvation was God's gift and related to faith.

"A man is justified by faith" (Rom 3:28).

But as James clearly taught, faith without works is worthless (Jam 2:20-23). Matthew also emphasizes that we will be judged on works to the neighbor in need on Judgment Day (Matt 25:31-46).

In this context our faith in the Eucharist must lead to good works. And our good works must be permeated by the faith which grows through love and the Eucharist. As we pointed out earlier, St. Peter Julian Eymard exemplified the need for the Eucharist to lead us to good works done for the poor.

Celebrating the Eucharist in the context of the gift of self, of contemplation and action, of proclamation - liberation - communion, we cannot but move in the direction of faith acting in love.

The Eucharistic Congress of 1976 developed the theme of feeding the hungers of the human family. Liberation theology emphasizes the eucharist of the poor: bringing bread to the hungry, because we have been fed by the Bread of Life. We believe we touch here the very heart of eucharistic spirituality.

If faith requires action, liturgy requires life, and contemplation requires that our contemplation lead us to the service of others, then Eucharist must lead us to a fundamental option for the poor carried out in works to all those in need.

Conclusion

We bring our study to its conclusion with a full realization that we have touched only a few of the many facets of eucharistic spirituality. Much more needs to be studied and written. The ecumenical perception of spirituality is only beginning to unfold. Yet we hope that the time and effort spent in this work will be a beginning and an inspiration to others to continue to explore the riches of eucharistic spirituality in our day. The Vatican Council has renewed eucharistic theology abundantly. Agreed statements both bi-lateral and multi-lateral give new insight into the theology of the Eucharist and Christian spirituality. We need to explore them all and frequently.

Especially do we need the climate of dialogue whereby Christians can enrich one another by their personal experience of God and our Savior Jesus Christ. St. Teresa of Avila said that friends of God must become friends. God speaks to us so that we may speak to each other about God.

We have written for a Christian audience, conscious of the fact that many of our friends are from other religious traditions. There is much to be gleaned from "ecumenical ecumenism" and interreligious dialogue as well. Unfortunately such a dialogue could not be presented within the limitations of this book.

The Sacred Congregation for Religious, in approving the *Rule of Life* of the Congregation of the Blessed Sacrament in 1985 encouraged each of its religious to bring to the Church and the world its rich spiritual heritage. We rejoice that so soon after that injunction we can respond in a small way with this present contribution.

We look forward to the possibility of continuing the work begun here in lectures and future writings. We write knowing that some of our thinking is seminal and some of our assertions may need greater development. We hope we have begun a dialogue and will appreciate the comments and corrections which others might suggest.

Bibliographic References

Alighieri, Dante. *The Divine Comedy. Hell, Purgatory, Paradise.* Trans. by Henry F. Cary. With introduction and notes. New York, Collier, 1909 (Harvard Classics 20).

Anglican-Roman Catholic International Commission *The Final Report.* Washington, Office of Publishing Services, U.S. Catholic Conference, 1982. (Cincinnati, Forward Movement Publications.)

Barta, Russell. "Liberation: U.S. Style." *America* 152 (1985) 297–300, April 13.

Beaupere, Rene. "Double Belonging: Some Reflections." *One in Christ* 18 (1982) 31–43.

Blair, D. Oswald Hunter. *The Rule of Saint Benedict;* with an English translation and explanatory notes. 5th rev. ed. Fort Augustus, Abbey Press, 1948.

Bonnot, Bernard R. *Pope John XXIII: An Astute, Pastoral Leader.* New York, Alba House, 1968.

Bouyer, Louis. *The Church of God.* Body of Christ and Temple of the Spirit. Trans. by Charles Underhill Quinn. Chicago, Franciscan Herald Press, 1982.

Bratten, Carl E. "Ecumenical Dimensions of the Expanding Church-State Challenge." Unpublished address to NADEO, April 20, 1982. Grand Rapids.

Brown, Raymond E. S.S. *The Churches the Apostles Left Behind.* New York, Paulist, 1984.

_____. *The Gospel of John.* Anchor Bible vols. 29 and 29A. Garden City, New York, Doubleday 1964.

Calvin, John. *Institutes of the Christian Religion.* Trans. by Henry Beveridge. Grand Rapids, Eerdmans, 1957.

Casel, Odo. *The Mystery of Christian Worship.* Ed. by Neunheuser, Trans. by I. T. Hale. Westminster, Md., Newman, 1962.

Chardin, Pierre Teilhard de. *Hymn of the Universe.* New York, Harper, 1965.

_____. *The Divine Milieu:* an essay on the interior life. [1st. ed.] New York, Harper, 1960.

_____. *The Phenomenon of Man.* New York, Harper, 1959.

Chesterton, Gilbert Keith. *Orthodoxy.* London, Bradley Head, 1949.

Code of Canon Law. Latin-English ed. Translation prepared under the auspices of the Canon Law Society of America. Washington, Canon Law Society of America, 1983.

Congar, Yves. *I Believe in the Holy Spirit.* New York and London, Seabury Press/G. Chapman, 1983.

Corpus Dictionary of Western Churches. Edit. by T. C. O'Brien, Washington/Cleveland, Corpus Publications, 1970.

Costa, Francis, S.S.S. "Communion Spiritual" in *New Catholic Encyclopedia.* New York, McGraw-Hill, 1967, vol. 4, p. 39.

_____. "Nature and Effects of Spiritual Communion." *Catholic Theological Society* 13 (1958) 139–148.

Cox, Harvey. *The Secular City;* secularization and urbanization in theological perspective. New York, Macmillan 1965.

De Vaux, R. *Les Sacrifices de l'Ancien Testament.* Paris, 1964.

Dictionnaire de Spiritualité Catholique: Ascétique et mystiques, doctrine et histoire, fondé par M. Viller, F. Cavallera, J. de Guibert, S.J., Paris, Beauchesne, 1957.

Duffy, Regis, O.F.M. *Real Presence:* Worship, Sacraments and Commitment. San Francisco, Harper, 1982.

Enchiridion Symbolorum Definitionum et Declarationum de rebus fidei et morum. Ed. Henricus Denzinger — Adolfus Schönmetzer, S.J. Edit. XXXVI emandata. Rome, Herder, 1976.

Empie, Paul C. *Lutherans and Catholics in Dialogue: Personal Notes and Study.* Ed. by Raymond Tremeyer. Philadelphia, Fortress, 1981.

Falardeau, Ernest, S.S.S. "Communion in the Spirit." *Emmanuel* 90 (1984) 567–568, December.

_____. *Eucharistic Service in the Writings of Peter Julian Eymard.* Rome, Pontifical Gregorian University, 1959.

_____. "Religion, Virtue of" in *New Catholic Encyclopedia* vol. 12 p. 270–271 and update in vol. 17 (1979) 562.

_____. "The Eucharist and the Communion of the Saints." *Priest* 39 (1983) 29–31, April.

_____. "The Eucharist as Invocation of the Spirit." *Pastoral Life* 33 (1984) 2–6, November.

Gros, Jeffrey, F.S.C. "Roman Catholic Identity and the Ecumenical Challenge." *Emmanuel* 90 (1984) 6–13, January.

Guardini, Romano. *Meditations Before Mass.* Trans. by Elinor C. Briefs. Westminister, Md. Newman, 1956.

Hale, Robert. *Canterbury and Rome: Sister Churches.* A Roman Catholic Monk Reflects upon Reunion in Diversity. London, Darton-Longman-Todd, 1982.

John Paul II, Pope. "I Have Recently"—Address to some U.S. Bishops. September 19, 1983. *The Pope Speaks* 28 (1983) 344–349.

_____. "The Reality, Progress and Problems of Christian Unity" (to the Roman Curia, June 28, 1985). *Origins* 15 (1985) 125–128.

_____. *Redemptor Hominis* (First Encyclical), March 4, 1979.

Kavanaugh, Kieran, O.C.D. and Otilio Rodriguez, O.C.D. *The Collected Works of St. John of the Cross.* Washington, ICS Publications 1979.

Kress, Robert. *The Church: Communion, Sacrament, Communication.* New York, Paulist, 1985.

La Verdiere, Eugene, S.S.S. *Eucharist: Proclamation, Liberation, Communion. (Emmuanuel* articles which appeared over the past several years).

Leo XIII, Pope. *Mirae Caritatis.* ASS 34 (1901) 642ss. Dz. 3360–3364.

Lonergan, Bernard F., S.J. *Method in Theology.* New York, Seabury, 1972.

Marmion, Columba, O.S.B. *Christ the Ideal of the Monk:* spiritual conferences on the monastic and religious life. 4th ed. New York, Herder, 1926.

Merton, Thomas. *No Man Is an Island.* New York, Harcourt, 1955.

Moltmann, Jürgen. *Theology of Hope.* New York, Harper, 1957.

Mooney, Christopher F. *Religion and the American Dream:* the Search for Freedom Under God. Philadelphia, Westminister, 1977.

New Catholic Encyclopedia. New York, McGraw-Hill, 1967. vol. XVI. *Supplement:* Change in the Church, New York, Publishers Guild, Inc., and McGraw-Hill, 1974. Also vol. XVII (1979).

Nunez, Eugenio, S.S.S. *La Spiritualité du P. Pierre-Julien Eymard.* Rome, Congrégation du T.S. Sacrement, 1956.

Orsy, Ladislas. *Open to The Spirit.* Religious Life After Vatican II. Washington, Corpus Books, 1968.

Paul VI, Pope. "Declaration on the Question of the Admission of Women to the Ministerial Priesthood." Sacred Congregation for the Defense of the Faith *Origins* 6 (1977) 517–524.

_____. *Humanae Vitae.* (Encyclical, July 25, 1968. English trans. in *The Pope Speaks* 13 (1968) 329–346.

Rahner, Karl. *Concern for the Church:* Theological Investigations XX Trans. by Edward Quinn. New York, Crossroad, 1981.

Royo, A., O.P., and J. Aumann, O.P. *The Theology of Christian Perfection.* Dubuque, Priory Press, 1962.

Schillebeeckx, Edward. *Christ the Sacrament of the Encounter with God.* Trans. by Paul Barrett. English text rev. by Mark Schoof and Lawrence Bright, New York, Sheed and Ward, 1963.

Schmaus, Michael. *Teologia Dogmatica*. Edicion al cuidado de Lucio Gracis Ortega y Raimundo Drudis Baldrich; revision teologica del M.I. Sr. D. Jose M. Caballero Questa. Madrid, Rialp SA., 1960.

St. Pierre, L. *"L'Heure" Cénacle dans la vie et les oeuvres de Pierre-Julien Eymard*. Lyon, Lescuyer, 1968.

Tavard, George. *A Theology for Ministry*. Wilmington, Michael Glazier, 1983 (Theology and Life Series #6).

_____. "Vatican II and Communicatio in Sacris" (unpublished paper presented to ARC-USA December 11, 1984. New York (Text available in part in *Food for the Journey* NADEO, 1985).

Tesniere, Albert, S.S.S. *Peter Julian Eymard, the Priest of the Eucharist*. Rev. ed. New York, Sentinel Press, 1954.

Thibault, Herve, S.S.S. *Saint Eymard's Long Retreat of Rome*. 25 January-30 March, 1865. New York, Sentinel Press, 1985.

Thorman, Donald J. *The Emerging Layman:* the Role of Catholic Layman in America. Garden City, Doubleday, 1962.

Thurian, Max ed. *Ecumenical Perspectives on Baptism, Eucharist and Ministry*. Geneva, W.C.C., 1983. Faith and Order Paper no. 116.

Tillard, J. M. R., O.P. "One Church of God: the Church Broken in Pieces." *One in Christ* 17 (1981) 2-12.

Tracy, David. *Blessed Rage for Order:* the New Pluralism in Theology. New York, Seabury, 1975.

Trochu, F. *Le Bx. P. J. Eymard,* Paris, 1949.

Truhlar, Carolus Vladimirus, S.J. *Antonomiae Vitae Spiritualis*. 3a rev. ed. Romae, Pontif. Univ. Gregorianum, 1961. (Collect. Spiritualia, 4).

Vagaggini, Cyprian, O.S.B. *Theological Dimensions of the Liturgy.* Collegeville, The Liturgical Press, 1959. Original: *Il Senso Teologico della Liturgia.* Roma, Ed. Paoline, 1959.

Vatican Council II. The Conciliar and Post Conciliar Documents. General Editor, Austin Flannery, O.P. Northport, New York, Costello, 1980.

World Council of Churches. *Baptism, Eucharist and Ministry.* Geneva, 1982 (Faith and Order Paper no. 111).

Wright, Robert. *A Communion of Communions:* One Eucharistic Fellowship (survey of the ecumenical relationships of the Episcopal Church). New York, Seabury, 1979.

Weakland, Rembert G., O.S.B. *All God's People:* Catholic Identity After the Second Vatican Council. New York, Paulist, 1985.

INDEX OF SUBJECTS